T0245498

LET IT GO

LET IT GO

Free Yourself From Old Beliefs and Find a New Path to Joy

Chelene Knight

HARPERCOLLINS PUBLISHERS LTD

Let It Go
Copyright © 2024 by Chelene Knight.
All rights reserved.

Published by HarperCollins Publishers Ltd

First edition

No part of this book may be used or reproduced in any manner
whatsoever without the prior written permission of the publisher,
except in the case of brief quotations embodied in reviews.

HarperCollins books may be purchased for educational, business,
or sales promotional use through our Special Markets Department.

HarperCollins Publishers Ltd
Bay Adelaide Centre, East Tower
22 Adelaide Street West, 41st Floor
Toronto, Ontario, Canada
M5H 4E3

www.harpercollins.ca

Library and Archives Canada Cataloguing in Publication

Title: Let it go : free yourself from old beliefs and find a new path to joy /
Chelene Knight.
Names: Knight, Chelene, 1981- author.
Identifiers: Canadiana (print) 20230509908 | Canadiana (ebook) 20230509932 |
ISBN 9781443466455 (hardcover) | ISBN 9781443466462 (ebook)
Subjects: LCSH: Joy. | LCSH: Self-actualization (Psychology)
Classification: LCC BF575.H27 K65 2024 | DDC 158.1—dc23

Printed and bound in the United States of America
23 24 25 26 27 LBC 5 4 3 2 1

To all the Black writers past and present whose guidance, joy, and light brought me here

CONTENTS

WINTER COMMUNITY CALL: BUILDING A DREAM HOME

Author's Note

This book is a space for soul work and dreaming. Writing this book was so much more than just sitting down with an idea and building a world and documenting experiences. It was an excavation of time, people, and places. This unpredictable journey has allowed me not only to explore what's shaped me but to let go of the things that haven't. I've now pulled from other people's history and layered ways of living and loving, and through this accumulation, showcased how Black folks do and *can* experience self-love and joy in ways that are as unique as our individual DNA. I want the folks in this book to be celebrated, and I also want the readers to feel seen and to take the truths shared here and carry them every day so that they too can thrive.

LET IT GO

A New Path to Joy

The Seasons as a Guide for

Unlearning and Reimagining Joy

U nlearning starts by first defining it for ourselves. For me, it means unravelling old beliefs, actions, and decisions that no longer serve me and planning the safest ways to let it all go. *What does unlearning look like for you? How open are you to the act of letting go?* By the time you reach the end of this book, it is my hope that you will have what you need to look back at the work you did—navigating the enormously difficult *unlearnings*, ditching old beliefs, and redefining language and relationships—and begin to see the markings of your own unique path to joy. Just the marking. At the end, you'll find yourself right back here, at the start, changed but grounded, on your path, moving forward. This was the goal I set for myself too, to come full circle. Maybe by using the tools I built—like learning how to say no with love, how to call back all the activities that make me feel good, how to communicate with those closest to me, revising my language, and most of all, how to let go—we can all somehow redefine what we *think* joy is. This is our destination. Y'all ready?

For the journey, we will need guides, and in a minute, I'll introduce you to them. But first I need to start with a big truth. My own path to joy has been blurred by hardship, but part of my journey is that I refuse to believe that *all* of my negative experiences are tethered to being a Black woman, even though it can feel like this, even when some people *want* me to feel like this. And when I feel it, it's a pain that swells and refuses to subside. I didn't learn this on my own and I don't think I can unlearn it on my own. But I'm willing to do the work. I want my joy as I find it; I want my joy as it comes. I'm willing to let the wind push me backwards through the difficult moments. Maybe there's something big holding you back too. *Take a breath. What is it? Maybe we can let go together.*

Along the way I'll be paying close attention to the micro-glimmers of joy tucked under rocks, etched in the veins of leaves, and bursting through the cracks in the sidewalk. I'll be looking for them! I won't be zooming past this gold, that's for sure. Slowing down is the thread that holds the book together. Look for it. Hold on to it. Lean into it. You'll find italicized moments where I check on you. You should also look for the bolded moments to harvest. Slow down when you find these. This book is not only the start of this journey but also a reminder to pause when you need to and investigate all the snippets of joy and watch how they have the ability to bloom into something empowering, something much bigger than me, bigger than us. I have tons of unlearning to do and it will be difficult, but the load will become lighter every single season. It just has to. Every time I let go. That's what I believe will push me to keep going.

If slowing down is the main thread on the journey of joy-discovery, then letting go is going to be the most difficult act along the way. But I've enlisted help. One of our wisest guides will be the seasons. Each season signals to us that we need to pay attention to our bodies, our desires, our fears, and our dreams. When the sun gets higher in the sky, it warms the landscape. Our bodies react. Like bears waking from hibernation, they communicate with the shifting seasons. We know that the end of a season is a direct call to start again and to make a new promise to ourselves, or to carry an unfinished one forward. The shifting seasons have the power to change our moods and perspectives, and from this comes hope. The shifting seasons also call us in to take breaks, to slow down, to say no to what's no longer serving us, and prepare for the weather to come. We can't sever this connection; it goes deeper than we think.

At the start of each season, I will call everyone into the room. I will hype you up, call you in close, and announce the season's collective community call. This is where the focus happens, where we stretch and get our preparation on! I'll divvy up the tools and we will get to work. And then, at the end of each season, I'll take some time alone. I'll move into my own private room. I will let go. I will drop small things and big things. You'll do this work alone too. But collectively, we can harvest. **Look for the moments where I slow down, pull up our bounty from its roots, and add it to my pocket: our communal basket.** There will be times where I ask you to slow down. The weight on my shoulders will shrink. At the beginning of each season, I'll offer myself (and you) a new set of tools to use. These tools may include affirmations, processes, methods, and quotes. At the end of each season, I will offer you, my readers, not something I've gained or learned, but instead a meditation on a few *un*learnings. I will lighten the load and walk a bit straighter, freer. You are asked to meditate on your own unlearnings and see what you can plant in its place.

Through conversation and solitude, I hope to showcase the broad spectrum of our realities and reveal the colourful kaleidoscope of joy.

My joy won't be the same as yours. This is okay. I want to tell a story, and at the same time, I want us to build one together. As we continue to preach about needing more space for Black folks, we need to also focus on calling in the variety of stories that contribute to the massively diverse experience of being Black. The experience of being Black is not singular. I'll say that again for the people in the back: the experience of being Black is not singular. We all have our own identities and can and should look back at all that has shaped us. This isn't easy work. As a mixed-race Black woman, I too hold a very specific experience, which I hope to unpack a bit more with each season. The seasons will remind us that we need to come together some-times too, gather our differences and slow down long enough to build empathy, celebrate, and heal. We can't do everything alone—even when some of us think we have to. Change hap-pens through the power of intentional community.

In spring it's natural to feel pulled toward renewal and rebirth, and to fully acknowledge the opportunity for new journeys and fresh ideas (just like this book, hello!). I began work on this book in the spring. The first evolution of process and sense of self that I noticed occurred not only when I unconsciously started to refresh my writing space but when I dusted off my boundaries (and how I communicated them), revisited my obligations, and protected the heck out of my writing time. The way I spoke was different. My shoulders were pushed back. My chest opened to the point where breathing finally became easy. I inhaled that gorgeous spring air! This was the first rebirth I witnessed that year. I was thinking, "Oh yes, look at me!" I tightly preserved that micro-moment of joy with pride, y'all! I have found that writing through the seasons has started to mirror what each season represents. So, our journeys to joy are cyclical just like the seasons, and writing this book is too.

Come summer, there's something about the warm air that pulls us together. The real nourishment happens, and you'll see what I mean when these chapters emerge in the book. Time feels infinite. The days, longer. We gather outdoors and refuse to hide our bodies, our souls, or our truths. In the summer, I want to be honest and say a lot without feeling like I said "too much." I want to be intentional with my language. Everything and everyone is visible.

Fall is all about planning, bundling, and preparing. This is where I will shed all the unnecessary parts of myself I've been hiding behind and strategize with the Black leaders in the room (more on who they are to come!) as we compare notes. But we will still be thankful for what we have and what we've learned about each other so far.

In the winter, we can analyze how the year went. Can we celebrate too? How do we repeat the journey and track our progress? I don't want to make the assumption that things will be easy from here on out just because we've completed one full cycle of the seasons. We will talk about how to repeat the cycle with new knowledge, less baggage, and new priorities.

In addition to the seasons, we have the guidance of a roomful of incredible Black leaders. I held conversations with leaders from a variety of experiences. As I opened my heart to their very different perspectives, I started to see all the beautiful colours that make up a new kind of joy. Kenitra Dominguez, a workplace coach for women of colour, validated my need and desire for solitude, as she too holds this boundary close.

Cicely Belle Blain, founder and owner of Bakau Consulting, taught me that the body, our *own* body, belongs to us and is worthy of protection, and it is up to us to find happiness inside of it.

Alex Elle, an Instagram influencer and self-care champion, helped me redefine self-love and strengthened my belief in the cyclical fresh starts we get with each new season. She taught me that the seasons of our lives are growing spaces. She looks at her own life in seasons, and every rotation around the sun, as the shedding happens, as the world around her dies, she is ready for the rebirth. I am too.

Alex taught me the power of the breath, probably the most powerful tool on this journey to slow down. I want to take a minute here to thank her. Full breath in, exhale. I found a friend in Alex. Even though we've never met in person, I feel confident in calling her my sister.

Award-winning writer David Chariandy allowed me to continue the conversation around the ever-evolving exploration of mixed identity. I can take my time. A lifetime, if I need it. Registered psychologist Meghan Watson helped me to be more exhaustive and reflective about the seasons and to seek out and rebuild a sense of self. Introverted leader, author, and coach Terrance Lee helped me see that my introversion is indeed a powerful tool and one that I no longer had to hide from. Chef Ifrah Ahmed ushered me into an intimate relationship with food and tradition. Writer Téa Mutonji taught me that self-love is not static and that it takes constant nurturing and questioning of self. Kenitra Dominguez also reminded me that Black female introverts have superpowers.

I learned how to love and not love my body through conversations with Cicely Belle Blain. Actor, writer, and director Anais Granofsky showed me how to reframe the most tumultuous relationship in my life.

I am in awe of our guides. But that's not all. I've also called in the words and wisdom of a few other late writers who still continue to inspire me today. Toni Morrison, bell hooks, and Maya Angelou: there would be no guidance without you! More recently I've also been guided by the genius of writer and academic Ian Williams, and to me, he belongs right up there with these literary greats who've helped me make sense of what it means to exist in the body I was given.

In the latter half of the book (should we call it the pivotal moment or the biggest harvest? I'll let you select the language), an unexpected guide shows herself to me, and I'll introduce you to Shakura S'Aida at the end of summer. If you are not familiar with these guides, that's okay. You'll get to know them here, but I hope you are inspired enough to seek out your own guides, literary or not.

In this book the essence of their wisdom slaps hands with mine. Joy strengthened through communal love, honesty, and hope. To each other we say, "I see you."

Now, for the letting go. Unlearning is often work we do alone, but the seasons can help us readjust our mindset, re-evaluate habits, take risks, and promote change, and our Black leaders can help us figure out the how. But don't forget, change can come at your own pace. *Slow breath.* Throughout this book, you'll notice I take a moment to breathe, a lot. I encourage you to call on the breath when you need it.

As you move through this book, and as you begin your own unlearning process, set your own soft intentions. Ask yourself what you need and what you want to call in at each season. Ask yourself how you want to show up. What do you need right now? Pay attention to the guides but challenge them too. It's okay if we don't agree or if we have differing definitions. Slow down when you spot these differences. This is where we can and should have conversations. Make sure you feel you have what you need in order to move into the next season. Sometimes we won't have what we need. Acknowledge that and just carry the work forward. If you have big expectations, toss 'em out right now. Replace them with the soft intentions. This is how we create room for the unpredictability of joy. It can come from the darkest of moments like a seed planted deep in the earth. Joy can come from being still and from sitting in silence. We never know what will grow from the seeds we plant, but the more attentive we are to nurturing ourselves, the thicker and more resilient the roots are. Re-exploring the work of poet Maya Angelou has really allowed me to fall into this understanding, so I need you to know you'll hear her voice echoed often.

Although there will be very specific stories from my past etched in this book, I use them as a starting point for excavating the joy, which means I'll have to revisit difficult moments. I hope you will stay with me through these. We won't stay there long, I promise you. But in order for any of us to begin the conversation of letting go, we have to reflect and look back. We can't skip this work. I hope that the conversations that fill this book will amplify the importance of celebrating differently and lead us down our own intentional path to joy. But reflection doesn't come easy to all of us. Maybe you don't even have a definition or a process for this yet. It's never too late to build one. Reflection is the ultimate way of slowing down. Asking yourself questions is the best way to get started. When you reach each of the community calls, I'll provide you with these questions to get you started on this path. This book is permission to let the light in. But let's be real. Experiencing joy *might* mean standing next to or in front of the upheaval. And that may be hard because we will have to look at older versions of ourselves that no longer align with who we are or who we are becoming. I recognize that, at times, this work will require solitude to reflect and unpack personal experiences that led to my own beliefs and values, and I hope it will be the same for you. It's quite the process to go back and pay close attention to the patterns of loving and unloving and what caused these patterns to continue. It's no easy task making space for joy even inside the depths of healing and pain.

Perhaps this book will lead us toward an unlearning and undoing of past societal mistakes as well as individual ones. Whatever you personally take away from this communal journey, I want you to feel held. Seen. Heard. Don't be afraid to let go. Release, unlearn, relearn, reimagine, and check in with yourself, let the light in. The fear will be there. And so will the pain. But in seeking out ways toward self-love and joy, we'll have plenty of opportunities, or shall I say, **moments to harvest** and celebrate all the micro-moments of joy and sit back long enough to feel the breeze of another season's passing.

You may want to have a notebook with you as you work through the book. I'll pause often and check in on you. I'll ask you questions too. This is my journey and it is yours. I don't expect to have all the answers by the end of this book (and neither should you—you tossed your expectations out, right?), but it is my hope that I can carve out the best route to my own self-love and joy, or at least provide myself a little clarity around what it can look like to love myself, so that you too can find peace attached to defining joy for yourselves.

"You, my dear, have a body. And should you desire to remain on this spinning rock hurtling through space, you will need a body to do it. Everything else we think we know is up for debate."

—Sonya Renee Taylor

Spring Community Call:

Affirmations

Here we are! At the start of spring, it's time to begin planting our own individual seeds of joy. We are all going to need different tools to get us through this first season together. My tools for this season's work will include affirmations that will help to see myself the way I need to see myself. My affirmations also act as a mirror—to look closely at my body and heart. I will call upon four things that used to bring me joy that I may have accidentally let go of in a previous season. Spring is about rebirth. Some things that die in winter can lovingly come back if we cultivate the right conditions. Your tools may look different and remember, that is okay. The common denominators here that we all have access to are the guides. Pay attention if what they share resonates and find ways to use this to permeate the still solid ground, partially frozen from the previous winter. This is the first cycle of letting go.

REMINDER

It's never too late to start building our own definitions of self-love. We can pick up morsels of wisdom from each other, and we can place them lovingly into our pockets and move forward.

LET'S FOCUS

At the beginning of each season, I call on all of you to ask yourselves the same three questions:

- What do I need or want to make space for right now?
- How am I really feeling? I want to be honest about my feelings with myself and others.
- What feels heavy? I want to try to let go of this by season's end.

1

Prime Your Body,
Plant the Seeds

"You still deserve love even if you don't love yourself."
—Cicely Belle Blain, in conversation with the author, 2021

I stand outside in my tiny garden, staring at the darkened colour of the earth. The rich blood brown is a magnificent thing. I can't pin this feeling to anything in particular, but I know it is time to attempt to bring this garden back to life. When I look back at my garden's history, I detect nothing but mistakes, bad timing, and disappointment. I used to think that anything green I touched would eventually die. In fact, this was the narrative I told myself over and over until I had no choice but to believe it. There is one lonely looking apple, a few sparse bundles of ultra-slender chives, and some magenta-coloured chard. The kale is abundant, though. So that's a small win, right? But this planting and harvesting is hard work. I know I should probably congratulate myself for getting started, investing the time, and allowing myself an opportunity to explore all the possibilities. I should remind myself that it's time to look at all the things that didn't grow and troubleshoot. It's spring, and I'm feeling curious about how the shifting of seasons calls me in to begin to reimagine my current path to joy. And friends, this is my first time acknowledging that this is work I need to do. Self-love and contentment won't just fall into my lap; they are things I have to seek out and build, things I am in charge of. This is the year, and the first season, that I start my path to self-love and joy, and it starts with my body. When it comes to my body, the seasons are my most important guides.

Reading Sonya Renee Taylor's *The Body is Not An Apology: The Power of Radical Self-love* was a good decision when it came to starting this journey. Her book asks us to explore the ever-evolving relationships we have with our bodies and the idea that "systems of oppression thrive on our inability to make peace with difference." But what drew me to this book was the way Sonya lovingly shared brief moments of her own personal experiences. To me, this showcased the value she saw in her own experiences, which was the thread that pulled me through. I felt like I was getting to know her (both old and new versions of herself). And to do this work that we've all set out to do, we have to start with the self. And while we're at it, we shouldn't be apologizing for all the happenings that shaped us. Some of you will be uncomfortable inside of those moments, and that's a temporary burden that you, my readers, will have to bear. Our guides are here.

I recall how, in my younger days, I would apologize for my body all the time without even realizing I was doing it. Imagine that! Apologizing for having a body. I remember how I'd pull down at the hem of my skirt the second I'd get a look from some conservative onlooker. Then shame would flower inside me, climbing my walls like ivy. I recall how I'd plan my outfits based on the type of transportation I was taking because I didn't want eyes on me if I was wearing something deemed "a bit much." The apologizing was a whisper, but it was there. I remember when I was the editor for a local magazine and I walked into the post office to pick up our staff mail for the first time. The clerk looked me up and down, gawked at my tattoos, big hair, and brown skin, and asked who I was. I presented my identification and told her I was the new editor of the magazine, and that my name would be on the pick-up list. She squinted her eyes in disbelief and told me that I "did not look like an editor" and so she could not release the mail to me. I didn't say anything. I just walked out. But looking back, I can't help but wonder, was my silence an apology too? Being the slow processor that I am, it took days to figure out that this was not okay and something had to change. Didn't I deserve to show up authentically? Had I ever really done that? The late poet Maya Angelou's words rang through my ears: "If I feel good inside my skin and clothes, I am thus free to allow my body its sway, its natural grace, its natural gesture."[1] Oh, how I wanted that sway. Let's get it.

For the first 140 seasons of my life, I unknowingly permitted my body to die from the inside out. Yes, that sounds dramatic, and maybe it is, so let me explain. Much like in my garden, I attempted to grow things inside of me that did not belong there because the conditions were not right. What do you mean I can't grow mangoes here in the snow?! I was stubborn in my youth. Tell me something can't be done and I'll try every way to prove you wrong. When I was young and twenty-something, I used to think that I would live forever and that my body would remain frozen in time no matter what I did to myself or what others did to me. I would be forever preserved, resilient. Ah, the joys and ignorance of being young and foolish. But I can't put all the blame on myself, nor can I place it on anyone specific. I can't say this is the case for all Black women, and I wouldn't want to make that assumption, but I saw very early that additional weight was placed on the Black women in my life and the pressure seemed to be consistently strong for every one of them. I bought into that strong Black woman narrative that I saw within my own family and externally—on TV, in music videos, and in books—and only twenty years later did I realize how harmful that actually was and how it affected every single decision I made. We have emotions too. We need rest too. We want help and support too. As a budding Black woman, I felt the pressure to absorb the weight of life's inequalities (in silence). But I also knew that there was more to this narrative and that I could be responsible for changing it for myself.

Through this journey of letting go, I could pay attention to all the smaller ways I was empowered every day. I could slow down and remember that I was surrounded by Black women and men who moved in the world the way I wanted to move in the world. They prioritized their bodies, eating what their bodies craved, putting their health first, and speaking to themselves in loving ways. This is what I too wanted. I used to think affirmations were cheesy, but when I saw how speaking positively to myself and about myself changed how I started to view my future, I knew I was on to something. I was changing the narrative that I told myself. Affirmations also help to increase energy, and with all the pressure to people please and shrink myself, dim my light, I didn't want to spend energy apologizing. But it also takes energy not to. As the first one of the four joyful things I wanted to mention, **I've brought back affirmations.** I'm not embarrassed to say I have Post-it notes all over my office that say things like "The world needs your unique energy" and "My knowledge changes the world." These small reminders push me forward and signal change is coming.

The spring season plays a vital role in the decisions I make, the conversations I have, what I unlearn, and how I collect and pool resources to share with my community. So what does this look like? Well, when the seasons change, nature gives us a signal or two, right? Depending on where you live, we know that when the rain slows and the warm air starts to take over and we can feel our skin responding to these shifts in weather, we immediately think about all the things we can do in spring that we maybe couldn't do in the cooler months. There are big changes I have investigated in spring. My body signalled to me a passing of time, too, because when something changes inside of us, our bodies ain't shy about letting us know! But in order to hear these signals, we have to listen. We have to rethink our relationships to nature and understand how to communicate and listen to the climate shouting at us to change the way we operate and move in the world.

The spring air has always smelled different to me. I recall walking to school when I was in kindergarten. I'd stroll through the alley behind our house specifically to smell the awakened flower buds on my neighbour's cherry blossom tree. I loved the glistening colours of the dogwood trees too. Those are the moments of slowing down I want to bring forward again. Let that be the second of those four things from the Spring Community Call that I want to bring back, cliché as it is, **I want to stop and smell the flowers without apology.**

Before I claimed full control over this wonderful vessel, the body that I now *try* to appreciate every day, I unknowingly let others chip away at this body piece by piece. I watched parts of me pile up on the floor into a jigsaw puzzle of shame. This year, I decided to call on my mirror exercise, where I hold my own gaze in the mirror for a full minute. I note all my features; I pay close attention to my eyes. Sometimes this exercise includes a verbal affirmation too. I've shared this seemingly light exercise with my friends and clients and felt the ripples of transformation that they've experienced. But for me, it didn't work this time around. I didn't feel any immediate waves. I tried again and again, like the character of young Langston Hughes in his short story "Salvation" trying epically to get a glimpse of what everyone else saw. Desperate to be saved.

Not being immediately transformed is not failure. Friends, we can't complete everything in one season, even if we have the space and the tools. Sometimes we just aren't ready.

The body is an interesting thing. We often pay attention to it only after multiple signs of something being wrong. A creak in the knee, the stiffness in the back, an unexpected twinge of pain when we reach down to pick up a small child. The body talks. The body changes.

When I turned thirty, I tattooed the last stanza of my first published poem across my back. I'm probably one of the few people to fall asleep to the rhythmic vibrations of a tattoo needle pushing itself into multiple layers of my skin. But it's true: there I was in a tattoo shop on the west side of Vancouver, lying on my stomach fast asleep as the words were being permanently etched onto my back. I had just exited an unarguably toxic relationship, and I wanted to take back ownership of my body, or at the very least, the pieces I had given away. This tattoo was my attempt to reclaim my full self and be introduced to the versions I hadn't (and haven't) met yet. I wanted something close to me that no one could peel away.

As I drifted into peaceful slumber, the worry narrative at the back of my mind did its usual thing. The unwelcoming thoughts festered. What if this fresh start would once again be temporary? How many times would I have to start over? This, friends, was the first disruption of spring. Fresh starts, indeed, but now I had to figure out *how* to move in the world with my body altered. I couldn't picture my body as strong enough to carry the power I'd just given it. I needed to talk this out, big time. I wanted to allow the dormant parts of my body to grow again, to fully flex.

I needed to have a safe space to discuss the body. Maybe some kind of an open forum—one that was NOT social media. For now, I have this book, this chapter, this small space. But then, I was taking the first real step toward self-love and, therefore, joy. It started right there in that vinyl chair with my back exposed. I had made this decision not only to alter my body but to give myself something that, once completed, was non-negotiable. When you've spent most of your life clinging to relationships, people, possessions, and beliefs out of fear of them being taken, a tattoo then becomes so much more than some rebellious act. The words I'd selected from my poem were mine. It only made sense to keep them close, and in essence, this tattoo then became a melding of the emotional, intellectual, and the physical. My body started to speak for itself.

It's okay for all of us to have different relationships with our bodies. I've scoped out all the Instagram influencers showing their post-birth bellies with pride, stretch marks and all. Smiling and showing their bodies love. I don't think that's something I could ever do or want to do. We are told over and over to love our bodies, no matter what. But friends, what if I never understood how to honour my body? What if I don't have the same support, platforms, and protective barriers as some of the women I observe on social media (mostly white, by the way) who force-feed me their idea of body love? But all of us have control over the narratives that we engage with, even if it means liking a post featuring a young Black father doing his three-year-old daughter's hair. The more stories of nurturing, love, and unique families that we centre, the better. Social media curates the conversations they want us to notice, but we can choose what we like, save, and reshare, and I tried to remember that more and more this past spring.

This season was still a fresh start, even though I couldn't bring myself to use all of my tools the way I intended at the beginning of the community call. But I started. I started to build my own care package for my body, and I started my very first conversation about the body in the safest space I could think of.

Cicely Belle Blain is someone whom I look up to as a writer, activist, and all-around supporter of bettering the lives of Black people from various communities. The body seemed to present itself as a natural topic for us when we chatted. The body is connected to everyone's path to self-love; we need it to get from point A to point B in that body. With this knowledge that the body is going to have to be an integral part of our journey, I wanted to think about how and when self-love is birthed. How does it even start? This is what I wanted to discuss with Cicely.

When I asked Cicely about the first time they heard the term *self-love*, they took a long pause to think. And I was in awe of this. The conversation had just started, and already I had my first learning. **Moment to harvest: Take the time to slow down. To just . . . think.**

"At first I bought into the narrative that I have to love myself first, but then later on I unpacked that and realized that it can be problematic because you still deserve love even if you don't love yourself."

I felt this to my core. So I sat with those words for a while. Was it even possible to love our bodies all the time? And while I am here, I may as well ask: Is it okay for Black women NOT to love their bodies all the time? Can we have a break and lean into this while still working steadily toward joy? I don't love my body all the time. And I don't believe it's possible for me. Maybe I'll gain some clarity around this question as I walk this path. If we can't love our physical bodies all the time, that shouldn't mean we are then removed from the list of those experiencing self-love, or as Cicely said, that our bodies and ourselves aren't deserving. Maybe we have to redefine love for ourselves. Ah yes, **a moment to harvest: Language is going to be integral.** Toni Morrison discusses language in her 1993 Nobel Lecture, and from it I've gleaned that language gives us what we need to move in the world.

Today I feel a certain kinship with who Toni Morrison was and the legacy she's left for all of us. I spot myself in her ambition as a writer, editor, professor, and mother. I found solace in the way she too wrote in various genres. She wrote what she wanted, what she felt she needed, and what the world needed to hear.

I remember hearing about her passing in 2019 while I was at a writing residency at the Banff Centre in Alberta. I was in the library working on my novel when I overheard two other Black women crying over the news. My body picked up their pain. I understood it. The body always communicates to us if we are just willing to listen. It was at that moment that I started to hear Morrison in my ear. That's when the guidance began.

Like me, Cicely felt that self-love ebbed and flowed and can be inconsistent and come in disruptive bursts that show up out of nowhere, without warning. We both recognize that self-love is not always going to be present in our complex, everyday lives, nor will the lack of self-love be easy. But hey, it doesn't always have to be consistent. We most definitely can give ourselves a bit of a break. It's okay to feel insecure and a dislike for your body. Maybe this changes over time, maybe it doesn't. But the one thing I am really starting to see and understand is that apologizing has been the most harmful action that I need to unlearn. In *The Body Is Not an Apology*, Sonya Renee Taylor says, "Sorry is how we translate the body."[2] Her words push me lovingly back into conversation with Cicely. When we talked about how we felt about our bodies in our twenties, we understood that time in our lives as like a second puberty, a coming to terms with adulthood. We needed time to catch up and love our inner child and those parts of us that never fully experienced love, time to do the strenuous work of loving multiple versions of ourselves and then letting those versions go. I think about my younger self. What had I promised her?

Cicely says we don't have to love all parts of ourselves. But as women in general, we are always evolving. The funny thing is that we can't always keep up with ourselves. Postpartum, I felt a lot of shame connected to the way my body looked and how it didn't "bounce back," like maybe I did something wrong. But this was simply me not slowing down enough to understand that all bodies are different. I had no idea that I was learning to love the cracks in my body's narrative in a way that suited me. But, still, even now, I do not want to perform (loving the flawed body on social media) and pretend. I want to show up unapologetically how I choose, and it's going to take work.

Reading Sonya Renee Taylor's words, I felt a warming in my gut. Like an extreme sense of guilt for how I've treated my body in the past. All my silent responses rose to the surface. When we think about what Taylor coins as "body terrorism," it connects all the ways in which female bodies of colour are violated and used as tools of oppression.

The Black female body has been under scrutiny for hundreds of years, and that's not changed much today. For example, open statements of sexual preference based on someone's ethnicity furthers our dehumanization. Janice Gassam Asare, senior contributor for *Forbes*, says "For Black, Indigenous, people of color (BIPOC) the fetishization of their race/ethnicity is not a new phenomenon. It is not uncommon for a person on social media to state their dating preferences, and while on the surface it may seem benign and even complimentary, oftentimes these 'preferences' can actually reinforce harmful stereotypes that are already held about different groups."[3] Our guide Toni Morrison also focused on the notion of race as "just a colour" in her final work of fiction *God Help the Child*. But as noted in an interview with *The Guardian*, Morrison chose not to write with the gaze of the white man on her shoulder. She wrote stories about Black people for Black people and without apology.[4] She was the master of highlighting the living and loving, the pain and hardship, and the power and success that she believed Black folks needed to read about. She wanted people to witness her characters inside their bodies, moving in the world the only way they knew how.

I hear Sonya, Janice, and Toni loud and clear, and they offer up a multi-textured perspective that I can add to my magnified look at the body. And I feel as though Sonya remedies what Janice shares by saying that "being unapologetic created an opening for radical self-love. Each time we chose to embrace the fullness of ourselves, some layers of the body-shame onion got peeled away, evidencing the power of every small unapologetic act."[5] This is where Toni comes in. By highlighting, unapologetically, the effervescent natural beauty of Black people in her books, she shows us a kind of self-love organically and without performance. A kind of self-love I know I want for myself.

I can't say how long it will take to stop apologizing for my body, but it's a large part of the work I am here to do. I'm gonna get that sway my way!

Resisting the notion of a beauty standard is a start. Whether it's being oversexualized by older men, being treated like women when we are still children, or being fetishized for our race, it's imperative that we define beauty for ourselves and do so via our own connection to our bodies.

Cicely shared with me that they had breast reduction surgery recently and that it was a huge emotional process. Having larger breasts had physically and psychologically impacted them since youth. It can be difficult for many of us to embrace our bodies when we are still learning them.

What does it mean to go out into the world with this body that is your own? We are looking for a place to exist. And this desire to exist isn't only necessary for Black women. In his book *Disorientation*, Ian Williams writes about being Black in the world, and I worked on my book while reading his incredible book. I hoped that maybe I could rediscover my own body, my existence, through experiencing his book alongside mine. Oh the guides be guidin' y'all!

Whether it was the destructive people I let tell me that I was not good enough unless I changed something about my physical self, or every person I allowed space for in my life who took a piece of me, I did not *own* my whole body as I should. Now, in this journey to and *through* self-love, it's up to me to put everything back together. In addition to letting go, stitching things back together is part of what I am here to do too. In seeking out a way to put everything together, maybe I have to look for the glue too.

I know that we deserve to feel that sense of freedom that comes from gaining ownership over our own bodies. *For some of us, we are already there, and if that's you, be a guide. Show up unapologetically because we are all listening and taking note. If you're not there yet, let's keep going.*

This spring let's start that journey and begin to tally up all the things that need to be dropped off, unlearned, and let go to make room for new growth.

2

Let the Music Move You

I can't help but smile at that little girl I told you about, taking a detour on her way to school just to admire the first buds of spring. Sometimes starting over includes looking back. Music started to play a role in my path to joy the moment I began to look backwards.

When people close to me asked me to talk about a time in my life when I was genuinely happy, I found it difficult to zero in on a clear moment, even when I searched every nook of my mind for a presentable answer. I thought my self-defined moments of joy, like finishing a new poem, finally clearing a credit card balance, or taking on a new project, were too small to verbalize or reflect on. To me, these were so micro, and the narrative I'd been clinging to was that getting oneself all amped up about the little things is a waste of time. Because of this limiting belief, I had trouble acknowledging clear, uninterrupted moments of happiness. I had to go beyond the

exterior to find what I was looking for, and my earnest searching led me to music. I realized that the pockets of happiness I
did experience through my access to music came as a result of
some of the roughest times in my life, but perhaps these were
things I could still celebrate. I looked for the moments of happiness that shone through demanding times. Just like spotting
spring's first buds, remembering songs allowed me to track
those moments and raise the joy from the past.

In 1997 I was sixteen, apparently invincible and so boundless
inside the music of the time, it was often hard to pull me out.
And I wasn't thinking about music through the lens of joy the
way I do now. Back then, music was a salve, a balm, the fixer
of all problems. Back then, I picked songs like I picked outfits.
Every detail had purpose. It was always a reactionary event.
And when I say "event," friends, I am not kidding! I recall when
my friends and I would record voicemail greetings for our pagers together using the tail end of a very specific song—selected
to pinpoint our exact mood so that the lyrics would speak for
us—and talk over that message as a way to let the world know
what we were feeling while hinting at exactly whose fault it was.
We'd press play on the tape player, lower the volume to just the
right level, and then when the part of the song that we wanted
on our voicemail greeting came on, we'd make sure we had the
phone by our ear, hit 1 to record a new message, and off we'd
go, changing the octave of our voices to a throaty whisper if
the mood we were going for was a quick-paced almost rap-like

message ... It might seem ridiculous, but this was what we did, and music spoke louder for some of us—for those of us who weren't sure how loud our voices should be. It's natural to feel unsure of oneself, especially in our youth. But finding even the slimmest opportunity for community and connection can look like this.

Other times, I turned up the volume on my Walkman, letting Lauryn Hill of the Fugees fill my ears and take me away to some place where I could be whoever I wanted to be. These are the kinds of moments I want you to look back on too.

Searching for small yet pulsing flickers of uncracked joy is now part of my reflection process.

It's important to figure out how music and dance saved me from parts of myself and led me to discovering the unexplored sides that I deserved to meet. This makes me think about the Spring Community Call and the four things I wanted to bring back this season. Let music be the third: **I want to bring back all the songs that used to fill me with delight.** This spring act was the prerequisite for the visibility of summer.

When I was in high school, my best friend was a short, white, popular blond girl who came from a good family. To me, it seemed like she was a natural at everything. Sports, grades, popularity, the full package. Her dad made us breakfast before school and when I'd go over on weekends. He placed rectangular hash browns on our plate, and I remember thinking that it was an act of love. I felt joy in those moments. When we'd go out either to a party or the mall, my friend would always open up her closet to me and let me pick out scarves and purses to go along with whatever drab outfit I had on. She was always trying to help, that was just in her veins, and it never felt performative. Another small spark of joy.

It was such an unlikely friendship, but we shared the same taste in music. And when she hit play on her tape deck and the glorious, infectious rhythms of Notorious B.I.G.'s "Hypnotize" blasted from the speaker, I knew I'd found my perfect match.

When I dream about spring, I imagine flowers erupting effortlessly, but at the same time, I grieve knowing that as soon as they appear, they are already planning their departure. I believe that people come into your life for a reason and for a very specific amount of time. Whether it's for a brief moment or a lifetime, there's always some bigger purpose attached, and sometimes it takes more than one season to witness it, to feel it, much like a good song that you feel in your bones. I learned to pay attention to pieces of myself through this friendship and through music. This spring cycle guided me into this reflective work. As the isolation of winter peeled itself back and the leaves started to return, I was reminded of the fact that I could indeed crawl closer to that full version of myself that I've been seeking for so long.

My joy doesn't have to happen in solitude. I discovered that music and friendship can help us redefine joy. This act of redefining is integral, and the guides have played a major role in this intrinsic reminder. I am not alone if I have them in my ear, but the seasons speak the loudest here. When I walk out into the breeziness of spring, my five senses come to life all at once. It takes real effort to focus on one sense at a time. There is a tingle of comradery in that.

Looking back, I can admit that making those voice recordings for our pagers was a silly way to spend our time, but I tell you, the joy that was animated from revisiting the memory is something I never want to lose, much like the unlikely friendship. That's what I want to track. I want to turn up the volume on the brief yet catalytic moments that showed up on this path to joy. Revisiting and reveling in the vibrant memories is a *contributor* to joy.

The aliveness of spring is what tells me it's okay to change, to be different from the self that everyone has come to know. I've tried my best to focus on building bonds and community through commonalities versus pushing folks away due to differences. If there's one thing I have learned about myself it's that it is quite difficult not to compare myself to others, Black or otherwise. As a young woman who always seemed to find herself in non-Black spaces, it could be a struggle to find a common connection that wasn't forced. But music was that universal connector, that bonding agent that said, "Hey, come dance with me," and "Oh, your moves are on point!" All self-doubt is released into the atmosphere. There are very few mediums that do this.

Maybe I'll check in with you now, dear readers. *Can you think back to a time when music transformed your current emotional state? Work backwards. What was it that made you feel that way?*

Music is an integral part of the human experience and perhaps even more so for Black folks. Whether it was purely to pass the time or to give each other strength during times of unrest, music can call us together for a common purpose. It's natural to want to belong and feel a strong connection to others, and music allows us that bond. But it's also just as important to do some reflective work and identify exactly what the word *belonging* means to you as an individual and what it looks like when it's fully in action. Can we belong everywhere and in every space we enter? No. But finding mediums or vessels for connection is what allowed me to move one pace ahead on the path to my own joy.

Falling into music by way of nineties hip hop and R and B was always a way to escape the heartache and pain of growing up. And although I definitely did not have access to the language to fully take stock of this, there was a level of comfort in knowing that I could rely on music to pick me up, transport me to some distant, far-off land, and even bring me closer to those I wanted to be closer to. I recall turning up the volume on Lauryn Hill's "Lost Ones" and Missy Elliott's "Sock It 2 Me," and suddenly, the cracks in the sidewalk filled themselves in. Maybe that was me using gratitude to power me through the tougher times: "I don't have [blank] but I am happy that I have [blank] and I'll use that to fill the gap." Now, it's not to say that music solved all my problems, but it offered a way to take a generous breath and refuel—again, that thread of slowing down re-emerges. I never saw this connection until now. Self-love and joy evolve, grow, and shape-shift right alongside us. *Can you think of a song that transports you to a different time and place? Can you let yourself sit there for just a moment?*

It took a lot of mindset work to get to this point, and I felt gratitude for my tools in spring—my mirror and my affirmations—because I knew these were the first excavators of my joy and that this work depended on me as its sole labourer, no matter how many guides I'd called in to the job. But I wonder how many people inside and outside of my circles are suspicious not only of the presence of my budding joy but of my desire to have it. I reread Maya Angelou's *Wouldn't Take Nothing for My Journey Now* and found myself mesmerized by the chapter called "Living Well. Living Good." where she tells a tale of her Aunt Tee, who worked as a housekeeper in a well-off white couple's home. On Saturdays Aunt Tee would cook, play music, and entertain the other house workers and her friends. The laughter would travel, wander and wind down the hallways. Angelou writes that the owners of the house would peek their heads in, asking if they could simply watch. They wanted to witness their joy. Angelou reflects on the fact that this couple had this big house, a swimming pool, and multiple cars, but they had no joy. There's a sadness there that I don't think I'm able to articulate. But I can say that this will never be me. I never want to observe joy only from the outside, never fully feeling in control of my own.

But maybe there was another reason this couple couldn't turn away from the vibrant and boisterous displays of joy Aunt Tee and her friends were exhibiting. Maybe some people just do not want to see Black people inside of happiness. Some folks also make the assumption that any joy we experience that is not tethered to the helping hand of a white person is unearned or, dare I say, inauthentic. As quoted in an article on Black joy in *FASHION*, Andray Domise said, "There is a certain level of suspiciousness that white people have when they don't get things. When you see Black people enjoying something, and you can't own or consume it yourself, it's like 'they're having all this fun without me, I have to go ruin this.'"[6] I gotta say, I agree with that statement to some extent, but there's so much unpacking to do here too because it's possible that we could interpret that statement to assume this of all white people. When I think back to that unexpected friendship and how we both shared joy at the same time, that was simply us existing together. Music contributed to my joy because it was a way to breathe and lean into all the unique folds that made me *me*. *Can music do this for you too?* These simple acts add to my joy inventory and they can for you too.

Music was also a way for my family, who all come with varying values, ethics, and ways of living, to leave all opposing ideas and beliefs at the door and just be in the moment. And that's really what music can do: it can allow you to be absolutely present. This was all it took to bring us together when I was young. And in those few moments, no one was thinking about how differently someone else was parenting their children or how so and so always leaves early, or some other comparison or critique. In the moments of music and dance, we were happy.

Music can tell a story. Music can soothe. Music can bring on a string of memories. Music reminds us that life is living. As a young girl, I recall watching the women in my family dance together at almost every family gathering and how in those moments, the world's turmoil dissipated. I didn't realize it then, but that was joy: The moments of existing inside the now. The moments where everyone's strength was piled together. Everyone magically knew the words and the steps. I often wanted to join in, but I also lacked self-trust and didn't want anyone to question my impulse.

Music can also showcase the linear downfall of a person's life. I think about all the documentaries I've seen featuring famous Black musicians such as Billie Holiday and Nina Simone. We've figured out how music was a natural outlet for both, breaking barriers and climbing to the top. But they were at the top alone, unprepared to carry the weight and the pressure. But they were activists too. They carried more. Was joy there? Was there anyone to bear witness? These women fell long and hard, and we all watched and bowed our heads. So although music can indeed be a part of the spark that lights that fireball of joy in so many of us, it can also be a reminder that the pressures of life are real and we all need to admit when things are getting too heavy. As spring becomes all-encompassing, I am seeing that I can really dive into what self-love means for me. This work is so personal to me and my experiences, but the folks I've called into the room help to show me a different way to let my hips sway to the rhythm of my fave song playing on the radio. *Can you find a moment to dance too?*

The Black guides whom I connected with shared with me how they've taken the time to learn the steps too, and together we can decide to press replay on that tape deck, or skip to another song, or at least that's what I took away from our chats. But there is no one-size-fits-all answer to how to love or how to experience joy, and I am slowly starting to be okay with that.

I can decide to press rewind on that tape deck, or maybe skip ahead and let my hips sway to the rhythm of my favorite song. If I can leave you with anything right here in this moment, it's that music can transport, be a balm, elevate emotions, and fill you up. Call it in, hold it close.

3

You Can Serve Up Your Own Recipe for Love

"Food in the hands of Black people is literally magic."
—Ifrah Ahmed, in conversation with the author, 2021

Much like joy, love is complex. Love of self, love of friends, love of family, love of the natural world. All the differently shaped layers, the temporariness of love, the permanency of it, the unpredictability of it, the loss of it, the complete immersion in it. There is so much to spread out on the kitchen counter. But spring asks all of us to pay attention to the signals around us, especially as gardens start to provide nourishment. There's no denying the way the soil is disturbed by the inevitable seedlings that push through the earth.

I have always connected love to the preparation of food because, just like with writing, I communicate *through* cooking. Cooking is how I speak all the things I don't always have the words for. Food is the perfect lens through which to carve out this self-love path, but I won't lie, I was initially apprehensive about writing this chapter (this came up a lot, by the way) because my own relationship with food has been uncontrolled for years. When I was young, lack of food was an issue in my everyday life—not having enough of it, fear of running out of it, the shame and guilt attached to being a picky eater when I knew I should just eat everything on my plate without question. If I slowed down to think about the food in front of me or pushed it around on my plate out of curiosity, I was told to stop playing with my food and hurry up and eat. I was taught to believe that food was there to fill you up. It wasn't supposed to be an experience. But is there room to let this go? Can I rebuild my relationship with food for myself now?

It took me 120 seasons to start the process of unlearning that food is only meant to be fuel. I wanted to rewrite food into my daily life. Food could be creativity, love, communication, and joy. Remember, I said there would be some major unlearning happening here too. Food for me today is a huge source of joy. As an adult making my own decisions, I have access to all the foods I need in order to fully honour my body. I don't like to take that for granted. None of us should.

I wanted to have control of what I put inside my body. And just like in the body chapter, I can't ignore the desire to have control over my movements and actions in a world that wants to tell me what I should and should not eat, spend time and money on, a world that wants to tell me how to be and where my place is. Cooking, for me now, is an opportunity for unstructured play—which very well may be why I am so opposed to using recipes. I love the idea that I can create something without rules and that making mistakes is part of the process. I can assess and reassess what works and what doesn't. The more I fell into this unstructured play, the more cooking became an even bigger part of my joy, and it helped me to deduce that although food was problematic when I was younger, it didn't have to stay that way. It was never too late to begin to reshape my relationship with food.

But re-establishing a healthy and sustainable connection with food meant I had to call on self-trust again. Self-trust is something that can develop over time—that's a bold statement, I know—but in order for it to flower, you need to use every single one of your tools without apology. For me, self-trust means that when I say no, it's no. Self-trust means holding my non-negotiables and priorities close. Unlearning and letting go are probably the biggest, most explosive acts of self-trust of them all. To start this work of building a more intentional relationship with food, I had to trust myself just enough to sit down and revisit my relationship with money first. Learning that the two were linked was incredibly eye-opening. *If this resonates, slow down and investigate.*

Food and my relationship with creating meals is one hundred percent connected to money. The best financial decision I made this season was to forgive myself for all of the past money mistakes. Forgiveness didn't just happen. It strengthened the more I figured out what was behind every money blunder, and that these mistakes could help me push forward instead of holding me back. But it was up to me. I looked at each mistake like a bridge. I needed to walk over each mistake to get to the other side. And if the weather shifted and I found myself in the middle of the bridge during a heavy spring rain, I would know it was a test, a challenge. Now, I could either run and hide to avoid getting soaked, or I could continue my walk trusting that the weather was temporary, reminding myself that the warmth was coming. I had to trust myself to walk through that rain versus avoiding it or, worse, blaming myself for not having an umbrella.

Whether it was buying something I didn't need, giving beyond my means, doing work for free, or even taking on clients who didn't align with my business's values and ethics, I started the process of forgiving myself. I built a loving process for the monthly financial work I needed to do as a small-business owner, homeowner, and someone with uncertain income. Instead of moving through money management with avoidance and dread, I flipped the script. I used the tools I had been gifted by the Black leaders and from the folks in my life who'd been championing me from day one. I built a monthly two-hour "money love" session into my calendar, which was a way for me to build in positive language and attach it to my money processes. I created a list of financial tasks, and I was careful about the language. I wasn't "paying bills," I was "investing in tools." I wasn't "processing payroll," I was "helping my community get *their* tools." I wasn't "cutting expenses," I was "spending intentionally." In addition to the regular financial moves, I now also celebrate successes, and I schedule this, I prioritize it, I protect this time. I pour myself a glass of wine as I dream of my future. I open my financial reports in QuickBooks and I vocalize my wins. I feel powerful here. Joy is showing itself in the most terrifying of tasks. Growth, growth, and more growth, and y'all know I'm tracking this. *Can you see yourselves here?*

This money love was the catalyst to building a new, loving relationship with food. But this was not easy. There was (and is) so much shame attached to past money mistakes and to past living situations where food was something we worried about daily. But looking for glimmers between the folds of pain was integral to forgiveness, trust, and increasing love. This was part of the goal: to remember to find pieces of joy wherever I could. The best way out of the shame for me was to watch and change my language. Language and mindset work is important in this book, so you're going to discover that this comes up more often the further you progress. But it's true: the way I spoke to myself, about myself, helped the shame loosen in preparation to leave my body. I wanted so desperately to pull these weeds from my garden. I was ready to let the wind take them. I was ready to let them go.

Once I decided to make these changes, I hoped I was ready to see myself. I shoved my hand in my pocket and took out my mirror. I flipped it open and looked at myself again. There were still so many weeds, but I could see more of the vibrant green lushness of a garden in progress.

———

I was invigorated by this growth, and I could envision myself celebrating in that moment. I was motivated to find more ways to forgive myself. Holding on tightly to this new-found approach to money and food, I didn't need to apologize if I spent a bit more on ingredients that appealed to me. I let go of the guilt attached to spending more than I should and not shopping around for the best deals. I value my time now, and I'm so not interested in spending hours shopping around only to save thirty cents on a pound of irregular cut bacon. Is that *really* the best use of my time?

Every Sunday I make my family breakfast. Nothing fancy, just your basic bacon, eggs, toast, and fruit kinda deal. The difference here is that I make the food at a time that works for *me*, because the weekends are my only writing days. I put out plates, cups, and cutlery, and leave everything on the counter. A self-serve offering. Everyone in my house likes to eat at different times and we all respect that. Sometimes we share space at the table; other times we smile knowing someone who had just eaten before us saved a portion sitting warm in the pan. Or someone else left a napkin out. Simple things. No obligatory moves for us. Not anymore. Joy again. Cooking as communication. *How can you use food in a new way?* This leads me to the final joyful activity in my list of four that I wanted to bring back: **Sunday food prep!**

Food is obviously so much more than just sustenance and I've been working on growing this knowledge every chance I get. Cooking is communication, as I said, and self-expression (much like writing). To create, to experiment, to await the most satisfying outcome, to show those close to you love at its most concentrated—this is what I am after when I walk into my kitchen. Creation, time, paying attention: important in the writing process and incredibly valuable when preparing food that you are about to put into your body—the vessel for this creative work. Wild how I didn't establish that connection before!

I didn't always realize how intimate a relationship we could have with food. Although it's an almost faded or eroded memory, I can still recall my grandmother working at her brown kitchen table, pounding floured discs of dough that she had spread out over the entire table for her homemade burritos filled with ground beef, potatoes, and her secret spices. It was almost as if there was this unspoken agreement between her and the act. A conversation was taking place through her hands. Although I have no idea what she was thinking when pounding that dough, I look back now and discern that intimacy, that connection, the rhythm. *Consider your own moments of watching food prepared. What did you notice?*

When I use my own hands to cook, I am touching and feeling. I am inhaling vibrant and bold spices, crushing seeds into a fine powder. I'm testing readiness between my fingers. My tongue tells me what to add next or what to step back from adding. Tell me this is not unbelievably intimate. Cooking, for me, has always been poetry. And with every new creation, I recall past successes and failures. I remember when the recipe wasn't right and I revise it the next time. The body holds memory in a unique way. But when I think about how my mother used to cook for us, I don't recall ever witnessing her process. She'd always have things done by the time my brother and I got home from school. If she wasn't there, we'd create our own meals. I didn't notice the conversation happening through the hands. Her relationship to food wasn't the same as mine. We didn't comprehend food in the same way.

Though that's not to say that she didn't talk to us through food. My mom is a very generous person, although she may not perceive it that way. But I noticed. I paid attention. At times, cooking was her only offering. It was an exchange. Cooking, for her, was a translation language. She *can* say "I love you" or "I am in a good mood" through the handing over of food. My mom is the first one to call folks over and offer to cook something for them, whether she has all the ingredients or not. She will figure it out. She's also not shy about asking others to contribute or chip in. She's bold! She'll say, "Hey, I'm going to make you this chicken and rice, but you have to bring the chicken and rice." I love this about her. When she stirs the pot, I bet she's thinking about saying all the things she doesn't have the words for. This is the common denominator I was looking for. I spent a lifetime withering inside with all the ways we are different. We were missing a shared love language, and here it was.

It's time to build a love language through food. It's my feeling that cooking is in fact one of the most nuanced ways to articulate Blackness. Through cooking, we can highlight the recipes, kitchen lingo, and passed-down processes that we've learned from our families. And if this isn't something we've experienced, we have an opportunity to start. My conversation with chef Ifrah Ahmed, owner of Milk + Myrrh pop-up shop, helped shape my new outlook on food and traditions.

After connecting with Ifrah and reading her gorgeous, poetic piece in *The Washington Post* about a Somali-style afternoon break for tea and sweets (casariyo), I felt inspired to start my own traditions. Just because I was not raised with a specific tradition around food or rest, I could start my own version of casariyo now, for myself and for my partner and my adult son. I could even take this one step further and create a routine connected with food for myself, just for me. Maybe I could allow my hands to tear into a dense loaf of bread, pull off a piece, and put it on one of my favourite plates. Maybe I could pour myself one of those rich espressos that I like. Maybe I could place both in the corner window of my house, turn the wingback armchair to face the window, and watch the mountains stand tall for me, proud of me for being present with myself and respecting my soul enough to know that no one else can steal the moments I give myself where, as Ifrah calls it, "my hands move with memory."[7] Why the heck did I think it was too late?

Writing about casariyo allowed Ifrah to connect food and traditions to the notion of prioritizing rest, which is something I talk a lot about in this book. "Rest is so respected that this tradition became a part of everyone's day and something that was observed by the country and throughout the diaspora," she said to me. I was in awe of this. So you mean to tell me that in Somali culture, rest is not only respected but it's celebrated? I couldn't help but then think about all the times I felt depleted or exhausted out of fear of resting and even fear of defining the word *rest* for myself. But rest does NOT have to be some sort of privilege offered only to the wealthy in the West. Black people—Black women, especially—deserve rest too. Seeing the links between food and rest has inspired me even more to start my own traditions. *Where do you see yourself building a new tradition around food?*

We often think that joy and happiness must start from the *beginning* of something. But sometimes those seeds are never planted, and yet we expect abundant growth. It's possible that we won't find the right soil until many seasons later. We gotta give ourselves some grace here and allow our fresh starts to happen when they need to, when the conditions are right. This is what the seasons are trying to tell us: to let go of outdated ways of thinking that no longer serve us and open ourselves up to new systems, traditions, and ways of living and loving.

I can sense how my ever-evolving relationship with food has shaped me and how it connects to how I show up in the world, but what does food mean to Black communities? As Ifrah says, "Food in the hands of Black people is literally magic. There is such a diversity in the entire Black diaspora of food traditions and there is so much innovation." I love the idea of innovation because I can see myself here. I find myself creating recipes in my head, building something that I can share with my family in hopes that it brings about a conversation about my process and my thinking. And food is constantly changing as our circumstances change. I've watched many of my Black friends change their interactions with food based on what was available to them at the time. Having the magical ability to rejig food based on one's environment is powerful, joyful. And this is where community comes in. There is a desire to share what we have. My own family is like this: we bring food together often, and each and every creation is different, not only in taste, texture, and process, but because we are creative with what we have. Food becomes a form of communication and connection. Sharing food created by our own hands is an intimate way for Black folks from various communities to break bread together and just let go (even temporarily) of differences. But having a meal with someone whom I have just met brings about a challenge that I never fully understood until now. I've come to learn that, for me, sharing a meal with someone I have just met is too intimate an act, and that I have to start somewhere else. A coffee, a walk, a story. The one-on-one meal is an act of trust.

As Ifrah says, "It is a direct line to everything that came before me," which I interpret to mean that sharing a meal one-on-one is like having my whole self on the table at once. I feel exposed. I believe the way we eat tells stories about who we are and about our past, and perhaps this is what causes the feeling of extreme intimacy for me. Sharing a meal can hold people together just like the common connection of music, but it can also highlight stories of the past.

———

If you're like me, you can't help but consider the social and political histories that impacted decision-making for Black people in the past and either broke or reinforced the very struggles of Black folks today. But I've been interested in how we've found ways to insert small cracks of joy into these difficult moments. I recently picked up *Power Hungry: Women of the Black Panther Party and Freedom Summer and Their Fight to Feed a Movement* by Suzanne Cope. This book is heavy in its truth, research, and narrative.

One aspect of the book in particular that made me think about the history of Black people and food is captured in the synopsis: "Aylene Quin had spent the decade using her restaurant in McComb, Mississippi, to host secret planning meetings of civil rights leaders and organizations, feed the hungry, and cement herself as a community leader who could bring people together—physically and philosophically—over a meal."[8] This description of a pivotal time in history eloquently summarizes what I've been learning as I write this chapter: that food in the hands of Black people is care. And like Ifrah says, magic. I close my eyes and picture folks gathered around a table filled with food, and for those few moments, their fears about what's happening outside those doors fades just long enough for laughter to fill the room. We deserve to pause amidst upheaval and breathe. Some radiant ideas have sprouted here. *Take a moment to breathe too.*

———

It's partway through spring and the seeds are planted. Through my own cooking exploration, through the initial conversations I've had, I'm learning that cooking can be a good space to make mistakes, an opportunity for unstructured play. I look back on the Spring Community Call and, yeah, it's never too late to build our own traditions. I can chip away at all these learnings and maybe my pockets can only carry a small bit this cycle—that's okay. I can feel myself getting closer to some delicious epiphanies.

4

Start Over and Write a Letter

"Writing gives you a second chance at everything."
—Téa Mutonji, in conversation with the author, 2021

The voices, words, and wisdom of other Black creators is what I call on when there's something standing between me and happiness. When I find it difficult to bear the brunt of the weather or when the day is unseasonably cold, I pick up my pen. But friends, the literal wind is shifting. As summer shoulders its way into the tail end of spring, I am paying attention to the subtle shifts around me and celebrating those mini-gusts instead of only paying attention to the big leaps, because remember we can laugh and smile and celebrate while things are in flux.

While working on this book, I thrust myself into even more reading and picked up books that had been on my radar but

I'd yet to read. One of these books was Glory Edim's anthology, *Well-Read Black Girl: Finding Our Stories, Discovering Ourselves.* I was floored by the way I instantly resonated with the vibe of the introduction and also how she seemed to highlight the presence of Toni Morrison and Maya Angelou. They too were her guides, and she too explored how she was drawn to the connection to self-definition and language. The similarities were so profound and validated the fact that we, as Black women creatives, *are* connected, even if we do not know each other or share some bond. We are connected through the desire to see ourselves reflected on the page and in the world. Our similarities affirm and align. There is such power in that.

We are all in search of "seeing ourselves" in literature. In the books our children read. In the movies and TV shows we watch. In 2022, at forty years old, I saw myself in literature for the very first time. I have Glory Edim to thank for that.

Up until now, I've naturally connected to female writers, guides, friends, mentors, you name it. And perhaps this is connected to the threads of self-trust I wanted to strengthen, but I find male voices speaking to me louder than they used to. Ian Williams's book *Disorientation,* described as "illuminating essays that capture the whiplash of race that occurs while minding one's own business," has become a voice in my ear that I've not wanted to quiet. Experiencing his words on the page has become more than an act of reading. I use the word *experiencing* to describe inhaling his text because, like Ian, I also value the sparkle on the page. I too want to call my reader in to engage with the text versus simply reading, absorbing, and forgetting. *Disorientation* is forcing me to look at myself, yes, but it's also asking me to investigate (or revise) the relationships I've had with reading and education, and the men in my life. I catch myself interrogating the role men have played and the various small ways in which I've pushed them away. But Ian's book held no judgment. The dazzle he created on the page welcomes everyone into this urgent conversation on race by holding open a door, placing a hand on your back, and letting you walk through at your own pace. I feel safe within the pages of his books. *A note to all of you that if you, like me, process things slowly, it's okay to show that on the page, in conversation, and through your actions.* Slowing down will serve all of us well, and I hope this book is showcasing exactly that.

Redefining language for myself is what has allowed me to feel a sense of belonging in the many spaces that I find myself. **Moment to harvest: I am so grateful to have access to books, writers, mentors, teachers, and other people's inspirational experiences and it's a massive contributor to my joy.** I placed this moment to harvest in my pocket. I may have stumbled late onto Glory's book, but finding a piece of myself waiting there was a big gift. Excavating, falling into, and exploring language is constant, not urgent. It's also okay to fear the seasons ahead, but let's recognize that there is a lot we do have control over, and it starts with language.

During a writing workshop, I challenged a room full of writers to define the word *failure* for themselves. Writers are constantly talking about what makes for good writing or what makes a book a success. Does failure mean you didn't sell two million copies worldwide, even when money was never a goal for you as an individual? Does failure mean that your book was riddled with punctuation errors? Or does failure mean that you ignored your gut instinct, your voice, and the intention for your book because of outside noise? Or does failure mean you never bothered to try? Creatives need to know when to listen to the clamour around them and when to just push people out of our ear. This, my friends, is part of the work I am doing this season, and I tell you, it is calling me into myself in ways I had never dreamed. Now, let's talk.

We need to pay close attention to the way we use language. How do we speak to each other? Do we throw around loose generalizations? Stereotypes? Jargon? How can we use our own definitions for common terms and phrases to call folks into the room in an intentional way? I've spent the last year and a half unlearning all the overused generalizations that I had been using as a rubric for defining and marking my *own* success as a writer. There is so much to unpack—more than I could ever include in one book. I've even had to look at the language connected to how I identified as a writer. A Black writer. A Black mixed-race writer. A Black Canadian mixed-race writer. What language is the *right* language? Ugh. Although I have bumped into some really complex narratives, it felt oh so good to start to investigate this! I've already started to build a stronger connection to my own happiness, and this arose from the act of unravelling and rebraiding language. Listen, I've been in plenty of situations where language allowed me to sort out whether a particular space was for me or not, even when it came to my second book.

When I first began writing my memoir *Dear Current Occupant*, I asked myself some serious questions: What did I want this book to *do*? Who did I want to call upon? Who did I want to reach? Did I want to write a story that was bigger than me, and did I even know how? I spent my entire childhood in the shadows. I wanted this book to be just about my experience and leave the zooming out for future projects. Why? Because I needed to spend time in *my* world. I needed space to understand it and to relearn it for myself before I even thought about calling others into the room. But in writing some of the really tough moments, I wanted to show the unacknowledged moments of joy that I must have experienced (although, at the time, I had not been able to look at them). And this is what I want for my joy today. To be able to connect the tumultuous to some kind of tangible thread of hope.

Maya Angelou's *Wouldn't Take Nothing for My Journey Now* is an eloquent book of wisdom and worldly observations. Her book is the epitome of living and loving, a timeless offering of what a life lived looks like, and it made me re-evaluate how I show up for myself in my own writing. It made me ask the question, How do I see the world and how can this evolve over time as I grow as a writer? Including so many writerly voices in this book became an integral part of my joy. It just started to happen that way and I let it—even though I resisted this early on. But after a while, I just let my heart receive what it needed. And that's the perfect way to describe how I feel every time I reread *Wouldn't Take Nothing for My Journey Now*. My heart receives what it needs. Although Angelou's book was published almost thirty years ago, so much of what she shares still resonates today. (Which reminds me, I want to create the kind of timeless work that is so urgent in its time and still holds weight decades later. Bring that legacy on!)

In reading her exceptionally simple and yet gut-gripping thoughts on motherhood, on being a Black woman showcasing joy in front of white people, and more, I realized (more than I had before) that, yes, I never had the language to explore what joy meant for me and that this has led me to carry around a leaky bucket of shame. So the question now becomes, How can I use the written word and the constant pillar of the changing seasons to climb out of the shame and find a new part of myself on the other side? Is it even possible? Well, one thing I know for sure is that I wouldn't be me if I didn't try!

Maybe I need to revisit the work I did in my memoir *Dear Current Occupant*. Although the book shared some dark, yet veiled, childhood experiences, that thread of hope and love I left exposed for the reader to coax out is actually coaxing work that I have to do for myself. No one else can be completely responsible for another's happiness. We can be contributing factors, but we cannot build the map for someone else.

Friends, I need a breath.

I'd not even realized that the exposed thread of love and hope was something I needed to go back to and finish unpacking until I typed those words. Maybe a moment of celebration here? See, joy *can* spark from the unexpected and the tough work. *Protect a moment for yourself right now too, just to acknowledge the work you've done so far.* **A moment to harvest: If there's one thing we have control over, it's how we pause.**

I've already spent a lifetime absorbing other people's pain—because I am a good listener and people often feel compelled to spill their hearts out to me. Holding their hearts—although a privilege—can weigh on me, and I no longer want to forget that I need to find a way to release that weight or let it go. Can writing then be an act of letting go? And do I have control over that letting go? And when I say writing, this doesn't only mean book-length projects. It can mean letters to myself, letters to friends or family, Post-it notes left for the mail person or on my bathroom mirror . . . it can be anything. But writing, for me, has always started in the form of letters. I used to use letter writing as a way to say all the things I had trouble saying out loud. All the things I did not have an oral language for. I've shared with you my desire to use tools often in this work, and we've already seen a few of those tools in action. Writing can be a tool. Writing can unearth clarity. Writing can be a bridge. To help you picture what I mean, I've made a list. The written word has helped me to:

- expose the many threads of love and hope in my mind
- create a language for my joy (this book!)
- have a second chance to meet a different version of myself
- climb through and then out of residual shame connected to this journey
- lean into my own definition of failure so that I could alter the language and redefine it for myself

If you consider yourself to be a writer or a letter writer, perhaps make a similar list. How has writing allowed you to form a more intimate relationship with yourself? Letters have always been the best way for me to fully communicate, especially when I was a young girl. I have a large stack of handwritten letters from my father through which, recently, our entire relationship has been built and then rebuilt. No phone calls, no Zoom, no in-person meetings, just letters. And the interesting point here is how there is no guilt connected to this. Neither of us expected the other to pick up a phone and call. Communication hierarchies don't exist between us as they seem to with the rest of my family. I've often felt guilty for "not calling" but 1) that goes both ways and 2) there are many other ways to communicate. Although we've been doing some *un*learning, we do have to learn to value creativity in communication. Text. Voice memo. Email. Other asynchronous ways of connecting. They can all create a new layer of understanding. With my dad and I, we both met each other where we were at, and from that, we started the journey of learning who the other is.

Through reading the beautiful handwritten letters from my father, I learned more about myself. Many mysteries of the self began to unfurl through our back-and-forths. I learned that he too is a writer, a creator, and he values space and time alone. (He told me that he built a mindset den, and I was like, OH my gawd, that's where I get this from!) And although he and I have lived separate lives in different cities since I was a young girl, coming back into a relationship with him in my forties is a huge gift. Through his letters, he has given me more than I could have predicted. I am starting to spot how all the selves I used to think came out of nowhere are partially attached to him.

Maybe I'll pause here to check in with you folks, because *if you can imagine a time when writing something, anything, brought you closer to someone, that's a nugget worth tucking into your pocket. Go ahead and add it to our communal basket.*

I am so excited that the work of this book brought me closer to him. If I don't come into any other revelations or explosion-worthy epiphanies at the end of this project, at least I have that. *You can slow down and pocket a moment of joy if you need to.* I don't think anything else could have done the work of pulling us together. It started from the decision to work on myself. The hard and difficult work allowed me to see that, just like I learned from Ifrah Ahmed, it's never too late to start a tradition, to build a path to someone or something and make it a part of your life.

While writing this, I revisited the intimate act of the handwritten letter. I challenged my nineteen-year-old son, who was struggling with transitioning from adolescence to adulthood while battling anxiety and complex identity work as a trans young person, to write a letter to himself exploring what true independence can look and feel like. It wasn't something he was interested in, and he wanted to just get it over with. (I could tell he was thinking, *Oh here's another one of my mom's strange exercises.*) But despite his reservations, he did the work. I was blown away by his letter. I cried, in fact. I wasn't expecting a display of his most intimate moments, fears, and hurdles. This was a rare opportunity to get to know him a bit more through this letter. He shared things I would have never heard pour from his mouth (a person of very few words, as they say). Even as someone who declared himself "a terrible writer" or had no affinity for it, he trusted the page as a canvas. His letter also reminded me of all the hurdles *I'd* overcome as a young Black female who faced some incredibly scary, life-altering decisions when I was young. It reminded me of the hard work I've done to land here and how important it was that I offered my son an opportunity to share. If nothing else, I wanted him to know that I too have been through difficult times. I wanted him to view me as having come out on the other side, fuller. I wanted him to see and feel the constant repetition of this work.

He doesn't need to have all the answers now, and it's a million percent okay to make mistakes. **A moment to harvest: Joy is connected to making mistakes.**

I worry about the pressures today's young folks carry. I try to be as gentle with him as I can. And he communicates with me in ways that make him feel safer, more comfortable, even though those ways can look different from the template we've all been presented with at one time or another.

The mindset and hopeful outlook on my life that I have now was not gifted to me. I worked hard to carve out a path that would get me closer to living the life I envisioned for myself. It was earned.

We are nearing the end of spring. I don't know about you, but I feel like I am more and more ready to let go and show the world a different, newly exposed version of myself. I've continued to look out my large office window for the first inklings of summer. The warmer days can increase our opportunities to bond. What is it about the sun and the heat that can call us all into the same space? What is it about the tail end of spring that gets us thirsty for fresh starts? Perhaps it's simply the fact that we can and should slow down.

But in today's fast-paced world, it's natural to feel the pressure to hurry up and get our words out in 140 characters or less. Letter writing is time consuming. In a world that moves with this quickness, how can we even justify the time it takes to pull out a real-life piece of paper and pen and sit down to write? But letter writing can rejuvenate, replenish, and help us refill our cups, and we need to act from a place of fullness!

In her 2021 *Forbes* article, Rachel Montañez says that according to the Study of Women's Health Across the Nation, "Black women are 7.5 years biologically 'older' than white women."[9] Imagine that! If we actively make the decision to try to reverse the physical and personal wear and tear that some of us have prematurely experienced, we can move the joy needle forward even more. I don't need a study to prove to me that life was and is hard because of how and where I started. We are all the masters of our own experiences, and these experiences are valuable. From hardship comes wisdom. Life starts can be difficult for many of us for different reasons, but we can stop, slow down, look back, dream forward, and allow for a moment of joy. Language, slowing down (my life and heart work), and breathing... this is where we begin. Joy can come from this. It has to.

I am making a commitment to myself to share the smallest of the micro-acts that have helped me rebuild myself from the inside out. We all deserve a space to just be and to exist, even when the world is in turmoil and crumbling around us. I plan to celebrate every single one of my small moments of brilliance. I deserve that. All Black women deserve that. You deserve that too. Some of the ways I've started to share my small moments of joy and success have been through voice memos to friends, during my weekly "let it go" sessions in my writing community, and with The Forever Writers Club. I also write them down on scraps of paper and put them in my gratitude jar that I keep by my desk. These small moments might include brief notes like, "I found a new bond with an old friend" or "I cooked a new recipe for a new crowd" or "I laughed so hard during last night's movie my throat is sore." At the end of the year, I'll unwrap each folded piece of paper and lay out all of the micro-moments in one space. Together. Just like these moments of harvest I've been pulling from the soil for all of us, small moments absolutely need to be valued and celebrated!

Writing is intimate, until it isn't. There's a closeness that can't be experienced through short, fragmented, character-limited bursts (sorry, Twitter!). In my twenties, when I would write letters to my dad, they weren't anywhere near the honest letters we exchange now. Back then, they were angry, full of resentment. And maybe rightly so. Looking back, I can see clearly that I felt an unhinged sense of shame around not having the answers to all the questions I had around who he was, who I was.

While writing letters has helped me build relationships, it has also helped me end a few. I've said a long-winded goodbye to the old relationships that kept me tethered to an old self. But now at the end of spring, I feel like I've done my work of calling in fresh starts. With summer around the corner, longer days, and heat on my skin, I need to connect with some folks who can teach me and remind me to value my own work and use it as a vessel to provide myself all the things the younger me did not have access to. Seasons and fresh starts, y'all. Canadian writer and poet Téa Mutonji reminds me that when it comes to my story, writing is an opportunity to tell it again.

But do I have the right tools and do I understand how to use them? The publishing industry that I work in claims to want to push out more books by "diverse authors," but what does this look like? What is the intention behind this desire? What kinds of stories is the industry sincerely open to? And is this a veneer or does it stem from authentic desire to create spaces in which stories by Black writers can thrive? Do we have to work through forgiveness before we can go all-in and trust an industry that, as I've said before, focuses on the stories more than the storytellers? How do we even begin to forgive? I wonder if, before we even look at forgiveness of others, we start with forgiveness of the self.

Téa Mutonji is someone who, for me, radiates self-love—obviously, this is simply my opinion, but I love the way she shows up. There's an energetic, playful aura I get from her. She holds a room too!

When Téa picked up my call, the first thing I heard was the crazy honking of horns and loud street noise. Leave it to the amazing Téa Mutonji to take a call amidst the hustle and bustle of New York City! She knows how to create that vibe!

Like me, Téa didn't *grow up* with the notion of self-love; it was something she explored later in life, which I don't think is a bad thing at all, by the way. We both struggle with shame and doubt, so when Téa talked about self-love, which for her means forgiveness, I was excited because I started to think about that initial question I asked that room full of writers: What does failure look like to you? I realized that failure, for me, means actively choosing *not* to work through forgiveness of self.

Writing books can be intimate. When we build characters, we can choose to give them all the qualities we wish we had, but we can also release that weight we'd been carrying onto them—the weight of being that person who absorbs others' pain, unintentionally. Writing could allow us to let that go.

Téa was so generous and concise when exploring how writing connects or could connect to self-love: "Writing gives you a second chance at everything." A second chance. How brilliant is that? "I use my writing to give myself a second chance to do all the things I wish I had done differently."

We know that we can write about characters who have failed in real life and give them another chance on the page. That's the power we have as writers. And when we discover and create characters who kind of resemble us, we are indirectly telling ourselves that we can live that second chance as well. We *can* get joy from this romantic thing we are writing about, without ever having experienced it. We could even write different relationships than the ones we've had. We can even write the relationships we wish we'd had. Téa shared with me that she often finds herself in predominantly white spaces and that she hasn't always had close relationships with other Black women. And this got me thinking about language again. What are we told to believe about the relationships in our lives as they relate to whether or not we experience joy? This feels like a summer excavation. I'll come back to this.

With this learning shoved deep down into my pockets, I wonder: Is there a type of quiet activism in writing ourselves into stories? Or writing our dream selves into stories? Can I pass the weight of my own pain and fears onto my characters? What can I learn from the words and wisdom of other Black female creators? In her introduction to *Well-Read Black Girl*, Glory Edim says, "Reading highlights the intersection of narrative and self-image to create compelling explorations of identity. Reading allows us to witness ourselves."[10] I don't know about y'all, but I would love to watch myself from across the room. Now that's a gaze I can get behind. I tried the mirror exercise again. But before I held my gaze in the mirror for the final time this season, I let go of my past failures of looking at myself and trying to see every glimmer of beauty. In this current attempt to see myself as someone who deserves joy and self-defined success, I saw a spark. It was small. Progress? Growth? Add it to my tracker? Is it because summer's around the corner that I see that confidence flowering?

For me, failure is in not trying. I write to answer questions, but also to unearth *more* questions. I am writing to try. Failure, for me, comes from ignoring trial and error. The joy I feel from figuring this out is exactly what I carry with me into the warmth of summer.

—

Spring *Un*learnings

LET'S UNLEARN:
LOOKING BACK IS A NEGATIVE THING.

When I look back and hold memories, I can find untouched layers of meaning, moments still worthy of exploration. When I look back, I can use my *new* experiences to see the past in a different light. This is how I lovingly come into a new self over and over again. If you aren't willing to reflect and look back, there is zero possibility for change. Change is dependent on reflection. I fold into this self because I can clearly see the old self as a bridge to get there.

LET'S UNLEARN:
HAPPINESS CAN *ONLY* FORM AT
THE BEGINNING OF AN EXPERIENCE.

I've started to see that I am a slow processor and that it takes time for an event to fully show itself to me in replay mode. I noticed that, in relationships and writing projects, if there wasn't an immediate connection or layer of understanding, I'd think that all must be lost, and I'd look for an escape route. But allowing time, slowing down, and preparing myself for the space to beckon happiness, no matter where I am on the excursion—friends, this is gold. Letting go of old language is connected to slowing down too. I can say, "Wait, that definition or word doesn't align with my journey. If I want to be seen and have my journey valued instead of diminished, here is the language I need…" Boom!

LET'S UNLEARN:
WE HAVE TO LOVE OUR BODIES
ALL THE TIME.

This is a biggie, y'all. Listen, my body has been through some things. And it holds pains that even I haven't discovered yet. I can't love what I haven't met. The love is gradual. The love shifts as I shift. My body is the vessel that helps me do this work. It's okay if I have moments of *un*love. I lean into that unlove most times and remind my body that love is always in production. It's coming.

LET'S UNLEARN:
WE DON'T DESERVE SECOND CHANCES.

When Téa Mutonji said that writing is a second chance, I thought, yes! I can build worlds I wish to one day see, I can construct characters that I dream about, and I can spin tales to create new narratives that maybe can't even be categorized yet. I don't have to have lived a dream to write one. I can relive inside of the worlds I build, and I can experience joy in the dreams I may never reach. Anyone who tells me I can't is going to lose their seat at my joy-recovery table!

What are you unlearning? How can you show gratitude for your tools and guides? What challenges can you create for yourself for next season? I am feeling lighter. I am ready (I hope) for the summer. Let's do this.

Don't forget to revisit the cyclical questions from the community call to carry you forward:

- What do I need or want to make space for right now?
- How am I really feeling? I want to be honest about my feelings with myself and others.
- What feels heavy? I want to try to let go of this by season's end.

"Choose people who lift you up."

—Michelle Obama

Summer Community Call:

Revising Old Language

Before we head into summer together, I invite you to breathe– Reflect on how the *un*learnings from the spring helped you prepare for summer. Don't skip this work. Reflecting is how we accurately track growth, or what I like to call looking back at our footprints in the sand.

Let's huddle. I want to share something.

It's okay if your garden isn't lush just yet.

In summer, I want all of us to focus on using our tools in a more expansive way but not to expect immediate results. Let that urgency go. Maybe we are feeling a bit lighter right now, and maybe not so much. Maybe we uncovered some new heavy pieces to our puzzle and this is why no two tools will yield the same result. My tools for this season's work will include paying close attention to my language: how I speak with myself and those around me. Friends, keep your eye on the way I adjust my language in real time.

Summer is about community and coming together, so let's consider redefining what community looks and feels like to us and how we can show up as our most authentic selves. I'll admit, I'm worried that I'll get too personal, too intimate this season. I always do. As soon as I feel the warmth of summer on my cheeks and forehead, invincibility takes over. Maybe I'll say things I regret, but I know this is the season to call in the courage to be vulnerable. And as per usual, my guides are with me. They are with you too.

REMINDER

Let's bask in the summer's heat and speak to ourselves with the same love we want in return.

LET'S FOCUS

At the beginning of each season, I call on all of you to ask yourselves the same three questions:

- What do I need or want to make space for right now?
- How am I really feeling? I want to be honest about my feelings with myself and others.
- What feels heavy? I want to try to let go of this by season's end.

5

~~What is~~ *Reimagine* Sisterhood

Summer is here and it's a glowing opportunity to show our truths, bare our skin, and maybe be a little more forgiving, especially with ourselves. Summer is the time to investigate the language we use with ourselves too. I know there are versions of me that *only* show up in summer. For me, this is connected to the way my skin feels under the warm cloak of the sun. It's like a recharge. The "summer me" walks with just a little bit more confidence. It's the version of me who isn't afraid to protect the heck outta her resting time. The me who goes out into the world, tries new things, and re-evaluates the people I share all my selves with. I take more risks in the summer. I try new foods, I get out more; it's like coming out of hibernation. Sometimes I even chat up strangers while walking my dog. (Hey, that's a big deal for introverts. Don't get it twisted!) But I have some big decisions to make about the relationships I currently have with all the people in my circle. Can my joy inside this circle be different? It's true, our environments inform our identities and our access to relationships, as does our own growth and evolution. Can I forgive myself for the past relationship mistakes I made? Can forgiveness be . . . self-love?

The people around me will continue to contribute to whether or not I unleash this powerful summer self. "We're oftentimes told that as Black women, we're all we have," says D'Shonda Brown in her *Essence* piece called "The Meaning of Sisterhood for Black Women."[1] But I can't say this is true for me anymore. When it comes to the work of self-discovery, relearning, and unlearning, I can see that there is more to this seemingly automatic bond that we are expected to fall into early in our womanhood. From my spring *un*learnings, I concluded that it's cool if joy doesn't happen at the beginning of something. But is staying true to an outdated way of loving and living keeping us in survival mode instead of allowing us to thrive? Let me use this summer cycle to look closely at the language I use.

Did the Summer Community Call speak to you? Summer is an opportunity to use exactitude to carve out an even more precise shape from the lump of clay that is our joy journey. But this precision work will be different for all of us. For me, it meant starting to keep a close eye on my language, especially as it related to the way I spoke to and about myself. There was much growth in my garden even at the beginning of the season. In a variety of spaces, I found myself stopping mid-sentence to adjust my language, and that showed me two things: 1) I was slowing down enough to acknowledge the fact that I was speaking in a way that dimmed my light and 2) the real-time language audit, or course correction, reminded me that this is forever a work in progress and hopefully inspired others in the room to adjust their language in real time.

The one thing I wanted to watch for were those moments where I was lying—and not big, bold lies, but these small blurbs, the tiny mini-lies that we often shrug off, the lies we think don't mean anything. For example, when someone in my community asked me how I was doing and I said "fine" even though there may have been a thousand negative thoughts swirling in my head, that lie of a response was almost expected. Even when my neck and shoulder ached, I said "fine." In community, in sisterhood, we should feel safe enough to speak the truth.

As bell hooks says in *All About Love*, "Widespread cultural acceptance of lying is a primary reason many of us will never know love. To know love, we have to tell the truth to ourselves."[2] hooks is so clear in this profound statement. I can see myself revisiting this community call for more than one cycle too. While closely examining the older, ineffective versions of myself that have been weighing me down, I experienced a vivid sense of déjà vu. I've attempted this work in the past only to arrive at the very same place. I've been here before.

I have recently been focused on shedding those old selves, but at the same time, I have felt in tune with myself. But that déjà vu feeling still follows me. Something has shifted in the past ten years. Am I missing the dependable camaraderie of my sisters? The folks I relied on just to say, "Hey girl, we need to talk"? Or "I've got news! Let's plan a night out"? The pandemic forced us to find new ways to communicate and to self-soothe. And once those of us who are introverts experience extra unexpected time alone, it can feel impossible to pull ourselves out. I know this has been true for me. At times, I've found myself stuck between two worlds and unsure if the bonds I previously had with my sisters had been broken or not. Sisterhood felt out of reach. It was like that moment, that feeling, that era... had gone. *Take a breath for yourself if you need one.*

Or maybe, it's time for sisterhood to be reimagined.

Reimagination. Was I grieving a loss of sisterhood or had it simply taken on a new form? Yes, language. I want to consider how you can slow down and pay attention to your own language when reflecting. Every week for fifteen minutes, I go live to my membership community for writers and I let go of something specific. After I've done that, I revisit my language and live, unscripted, in the moment. I call the other writers in the room into that act too. They watch me let go, learn, relearn, and reimagine, in real time for fifteen minutes. So let me do that here too. Maybe sisterhood has expanded to include people and notions that weren't as important to me in my twenties. I remember my girls and I driving down Robson Street, a small yet bustling shopping district in Vancouver lined with cafes, bistros, and boutiques. I remember us howling out the window at passersby like we had some astute advice for them, since we were in a car and they were on foot. We'd stop for appies and a drink at the local Cactus Club, only committing to the venue if the vibe was right and the place was full. We'd take our usual space on the small patio, shades on, smiles wide.

Maybe it was a simpler time. Maybe real-life hurdles hadn't found us yet. But when I think about the pain my young eyes saw in girlhood, I know those hurdles *did* find me, but that they sat there dormant under a large to-do list. I'd been piling things on top of my trauma for years, the weight of which I am now combing through. I refuse to skip this work. When we commit to this work of building our own map to joy, we have to expect random moments of emotional upheaval and a whole lotta questions to arise. We can't or shouldn't avoid this when it comes. We can, as I've learned, slow down and acknowledge and ask, "What is this really?" and then decide if we can lean in or if it's safer for us to lean out. So yeah, maybe I missed my sisters and staying inside and isolating had become the norm for me. But maybe it was time to step outside.

I've started to realize that sisterhood today, although intrinsic to my everyday being, is so much more to me than the relationships I had with Black women friends and family when I was younger. It's also the space where I can include other women who were there at the most ideal times. The women who show up for me when no one else sees the need to do so. The women who check in just to ask if I need anything. The women who make sure that I am consistently creating and working on my dream life instead of always building a blueprint for everyone else's. The women who let me be cared for.

I can't help but think of one of my closest sisters, Jónína Kirton, a Red River Métis and Icelandic woman who, like me, had to navigate complex conversations connected to identity. As fellow writers, mothers, and teachers, she and I bonded on many levels. I can't recall when I first met this incredible woman, and this is likely due to the fact that she has always been with me. As a guide. Another guide! I can't even begin to tell y'all how many times she texted or called me at the most perfect moment. Our energies have always been aligned in this way. My definition of sisterhood has expanded beyond the Black, female-identifying membership. My new definition included her. Maybe this is the reimagination I am pondering.

I've always kept my circles small. With so much happening in the world, we must remember what we have control over, and that what we consume, discuss, debate, and create space for can take its toll on our minds and bodies. We have control over how we react. I know that the sisterhood I build and maintain today will be centred on self-love and open, solution-based discussions. My sisterhood of the future will look like hooks's image of loving ourselves through truth-telling.

Out of all of the seasons, summer has always felt like the, season that empowers me to break templates, get outside, do something . . . extra. Backyard BBQs, hiking trails, vacations, outdoor music shows—there's an opportunity to move differently, and for me the confidence comes from knowing that this is a temporary, three-month period of "being out there." After that comes the very clear shift to fall, when I can go back into myself.

What does sisterhood look like through extreme life changes? *Feel free to take a moment for yourself here to investigate your own answer. If* sisterhood *isn't a word you use, how can you create your own language here?*

I should pause to mention that summer can be overstimulating for some folks. There can be a lot of pressure to show up and show out. But friends, this is where the mindset tools, the micro-moments of joy, and the newly reimagined sisterhood need to come through. Call on those unlearnings too. *What do you have to remind yourself of in order to move through summer with a bit more ease? What do we do if our seemingly clear path to joy begins to feel unattainable? How can language help us climb over these hurdles that unexpectedly show up in these warm summer months?*

In the summer, I spend some time acknowledging that my fears, worries, and anger have been clouding the current path to joy. But remember, we are all working through something big—one major, ultimate unlearning, letting go of what's holding us back—and I knew there would come a point when I'd have to face this head-on. Earlier in the season, during one of my live "let it go" sessions, I spoke about my own fear around sharing small successes. I bookended the session with James Baldwin's words: "To defend oneself against a fear is simply to ensure that one will, one day, be conquered by it; fears must be faced."[3]

I can carry Baldwin's words even further now and pause for **a moment to harvest: Because of my time spent redefining sisterhood, I know that I don't have to face every fear alone, but if I need to, I can have that space.**

Collectively, we've let go of a lot at this point and we should be feeling a bit lighter. But there is often work that we have to carry forward into the next season. When I consider the spring unlearnings, I draw again on the unlearning that looking back is a negative thing. Looking back can inform next steps, future movements. So how has the past value I placed on sisterhood informed how I move now? How can I use my past definition of sisterhood to lean into reimagination? Sisterhood can be the way I send for my Black women writers. Sisterhood doesn't have to only mean occupying the same physical time and space. I have so many literary guides, visionaries that I look up to. I can't discount them, especially when I think about the ripples that we can't always witness. Glory Edim's words made their way to me at the most perfect moment, and maybe my words will ripple out to the right sisters too. We have to lean on that this season. There are so many possibilities out there, and I know it's the energy of summer that allows me to pay attention!

I wanted to use summer to get prepared to release people and narratives that have held me back. In navigating the spring through incredibly nurturing and eye-opening conversations with Cicely Belle Blain, Ifrah Ahmed, and Téa Mutonji about committing to our unique definitions of self-love, the time came to put that into action. Ample breaths felt so necessary. Let's start putting our moments of harvest into action!

To do this work, I needed to summon Téa. I started to reflect on our conversation and the language we both used. Is there anything I would revise? When she spoke about not having very many Black female friends, I knew that there was a way to live inside of a different narrative, that the longing I felt for a time past could also be similar to the grieving we feel for an experience or relationship that never really formed. Téa often found herself in very white spaces and felt a sense of disappointment in not having many Black female friends. Again, we are by-products of our environments, but when I think of that reimagination of sisterhood, I know now, from Ifrah, that it's never too late to begin to expand our circles, our definitions, our traditions, and our needs, because this is indeed an act of truth-telling and, therefore, love.

A few seasons ago, I signed up for a fitness app called Peloton where you can check out pre-recorded workouts in every category imaginable. When seeking out instructors, I found myself scrolling for brown bodies. Then I came upon

Chelsea Jackson Roberts, a Black female instructor who mostly offered yoga classes inside the app. I pressed play. "What's up, Peloton! It's your girl, Chelsea Jackson Roberts!" It was her voice, style, and genuine attitude that made me first watch her A Tribe Called Quest yoga flow. Throughout the practice, she used words like *community, body love,* and *dance breaks.* I was, like, oh this is not something I have ever heard when taking a workout class. I immediately connected to my body, to my language, and to sisterhood. Hmm. I was alone in my living room, reimagining sisterhood.

What can it look like for Black women to be their full selves, their true selves, all the time?

I recall a message exchange with one of my aunts, someone whom I considered to be the most genuine person on earth— the energy that shoots out from her smile, the way she opens up her home to family and the community, how she lovingly prepares food for everyone... But I have always been curious to know if she wanted more. What if there were a side to her that she wanted the world to see but didn't feel safe enough to show it? I often sense this about her, like there's a self yet to emerge. Maybe that's me reading too much into the energy around me. Sometimes there isn't a language for something. Sometimes the energy is all you have. Can my reimagined definition of sisterhood include energy alignment? I really like this one.

Maybe we hold on to old selves and belief systems because we aren't sure where to go next if we *do* let go. To help myself visualize this, I picture the jungle gym in the playground at my elementary school and how I'd watch some of the kids in my class swing easily from one bar to the next, over and over. I look back and see myself hanging from that first bar, afraid to let go, uncertain about the path to the next bar. How was it that the others seemed so certain? But my now-logical desire to slow down is the reminder I need. This journey isn't always linear. As we let go, we may start to notice voids or empty chunks of space. Sometimes we need to get comfortable sitting inside that void before attempting to fill it up. I likely needed to go back and acknowledge these voids before I figured out how to go forward.

I am so appreciative of the Summer Community Call. It's helped me to work through some complex stuff. I am eager for the rest of summer. This work has just started and I know that these entry points into this complex work are just the scaffoldings I need right now. I have a feeling I am entering into the most whole part of myself and doing so on purpose.

6

~~Cut Folks Out~~
Revisit Loving Ways
to Let Go

'd like to dive back into that summer confidence I talked about earlier. Are we more invincible in the summer? Do our insecurities take a back seat? Perhaps. And my heart sings at this idea that we can fall into love and out of it without an instruction book or a long list of "ifs." The heat of summer preaches limitless possibilities. I wonder if this willingness to step outside with a bit more confidence is simply due to the sun's glare or the rhythmic pulsing beat of the music pouring through my headphones. As soon as the sun comes out, I feel encouraged to throw on a pair of shades to hide any sadness that might be left over from the last season. That unfinished business may be there and I have acknowledged it, but now in the summer I want to spend time outside and connect with the physical world around me. Love right now is imminent. Love is present, and so I have to release the narrative that I can't experience joy and love while I'm still working through sadness. And the language altering I've started has opened up a door for me. I can continue to move as slow as I need to. Not everything can be completed or wiped clean in a single season.

In her generous book on the craft of writing, *Breathing the Page: Reading the Act of Writing,* Betsy Warland lovingly taught me all about proximity and how being close to the fire or watching it burn from across the street could birth two very different perspectives. Leave it to me to learn about communication, loving, and leaving from a writing exercise on proximity in one of my first writing classes. I explored this in my writing, no doubt, but I took this proximity work personally. I thought about how I have often struggled to communicate authentically with certain people and in various spaces. Was it me? Or were we simply not giving each other enough distance? Can I love someone from across the street?

But before I even investigate loving from across the street, I have to cross the street. I have to retrain my brain to embrace a new way of communicating and new proximities–hence the focus on language adjustments. But I also don't want to run the risk of losing love. If I walk across the street, will this shrink my possibility for love?

We all express and receive love differently. For me, I've always paid close attention to energy. Whether it's the tone of someone's voice, how they hold my ideas or responses, or just how they decide when to show up, energy matters. I can feel nourished, loved, and seen when the right energy is around me and I've slowed down long enough to pick up on it. Receiving love and being cared for is a lifelong journey, but I think it takes the right gifter and the perfect distance. You don't have to be right next to me for me to know love. Love can come through a text, through a voice memo, and by not having expectations around what you receive in return. Love, then, is selfless and infinite. Love is showing your specific truth. Flecks of joy will always live here. But sometimes we can't come to an agreement about the proximity required, the perfect conditions for love to grow, and that often leads to misunderstandings connected to love. A not-so-lush garden.

Experiencing love and joy is connected to letting go. When we let go of things that no longer serve us, we are organically creating more space for the things that do. Let's think about this for just a second. We *can't* hold on to people, situations, and narratives that we know stall our growth. But we can still carry love for them in new ways and even from a distance. Loving someone from a distance can look like using new ways to communicate. It can mean not being as available. It can mean loving on your terms. And since the spring was about fresh starts, I feel like the foundational work to begin letting go has started. The ground is fertile. In summer, there's heat sitting on top of the soil. It's magnetic.

I know that I want to re-evaluate loving from a distance at the end of this cycle; this isn't something that can be completed in one season. I hope to give myself a bit of grace every season too. *Has your definition of joy changed at all? What have*

211

you unlearned about the action of love? How can you bring joy home? What are the patterns of loving and unloving that have followed you over the course of your life? If you have to put a pin in this, it's okay. Let's see how many seasons we all need to answer those questions. Stay with me, friends.

I planted many seeds last spring. Some grew into lush sustenance, but most seeds did not sprout. I may need a few more cycles to get it right, especially as it relates to connecting with family, including chosen family, and sorting out what love really is or can be. At the start of summer, I looked out at my partially grown garden, and a thin sense of failure seeped into my bones. But then a whisper from Maya Angelou showed up at just the right time: "Of course, there is no absolute assurance that those things I plant will always fall upon arable land and will take root and grow, nor can I know if another cultivator did not leave contrary seeds before I arrived. I do know, however, that if I leave little to chance, if I am careful about the kinds of seeds I plant, about their potency and nature, I can, within reason, trust my expectations."[4] In other words, we can't see into the future, but we also can't be upset about the results we didn't get from the work we didn't do. Maybe the summer is the perfect time to do a little bit more work.

In the first chapter, I spoke about the body and how I unknowingly allowed folks to chip away at mine piece by piece. Can

I explore this for a minute? Through conversation, reflection, and letting go, I know I've built up more self-trust along the way. Now is the time to investigate how defining love for the self is so integral to understanding the decisions we make. What are we after? When I speak about the body here, I'm looking at it through a metaphorical lens. This body holds. This body carries, but it also remembers. The body remembers.

Earlier this year, I made the decision to refashion the complex relationship I held with my mother. It was finally time to let go of that hope for the fairy-tale relationship I'd viewed on TV or between friends and their mothers. Although the fall will allow me the space to play with this idea, I want to think about love in the context of letting go and how love can be unspoken. It can be embedded in how we move and the words that don't form on our tongues—the way we don't always know just how to say I love you. Language—especially being open to new forms—will be what I have to focus on.

A few summers ago, I helped move my mother from her less-than-liveable basement suite to a townhouse in my complex. Sure, I was worried about how physically close we were going to be to one another (her unit was right behind mine), and, yeah, I predicted that my boundaries would get a little trampled on, but I wanted her to have a safe space to lay down roots, a space she could be proud of. A little backyard where she too could plant her seeds, watch her hard work bust through that soil, and smile knowing it was by her hand. And if that meant that I'd have to deal with some awkward moments, well, so be it. I wanted her to sow the beginnings of her own garden.

Moving through the pandemic taught me about distance and brought me closer to myself, my needs, and my expectations. We all know the feeling of being socially distanced for years, and this is a significant global connection, a common denominator we share across borders and cultures. But that isolation was felt differently by everyone. For me, it was a major opportunity to turn inward, to look at the years of scars and mistakes, and to unravel that spool of yarn one light tug at a time. Not gonna lie, I enjoyed being mandated to stay at home. It felt like an opportunity for the world to see that things could be done differently. Being isolated allowed me time and space with myself. All the old versions too.

My mom is vocal, loud. She asks for what she wants, hell, she takes what she wants. I used to be embarrassed by this. But the more I thought about it, the more I admired her for that. In her own way, she's always managed to ask for what she needed, especially when she could not give it to herself. But prior to figuring this out about her, I hid from it. I didn't want to be asked, every day, if I could do something, pick something, give more than I had. I just couldn't do it.

What was this, really?

The time spent in isolation allowed me to sort through our complex relationship and recognize that all I had to do was reimagine the way we communicated. I remember the day I first realized that I was in *control* of my own happiness. I had just gotten off the phone with a good friend of mine and we had been discussing some of the familial relationships that were tugging on us. The complex and nuanced ones. We trouble-shooted together, we cried out our truths together and caught them spilling out on the linoleum. I told her how I never heard my mother tell me she loved me in a way that made me *feel it* in my bones. I told my friend how I'd had this (unrealistic) expectation that the love of a Black mother was supposed to be thick and syrup-like. Warm and all-encompassing like the tail end of Vancouver summer days, and I told her that I didn't understand why I couldn't feel that. I told her that I didn't understand why I didn't *deserve* that. My friend reminded me to slow down, and she asked about my mother's own experience with belonging and self-love.

"When was the first time your mother experienced real love?" I sat with the weight of this question. I clamped my eyes shut and tried to picture it. A film roll of terrible memories flooded my mind, but no concrete image of love. Not even the essence of it. I've been trying to find the answer to this question for so long. I know it's something that many folks would say could easily be answered if I asked her directly, but it's so much more multi-layered than that. And if by the time I reach this book's end, I still do not have an answer for this question, I have to be okay with that and recommit to the next cycle. I was exhausted from trying to force a relationship that mirrored what I thought a Black mother-daughter relationship should be. I decided that for us to indeed thrive in a space together, one of us had to cross the street away from the fire. This meant that some of the things I used to want to communicate with her about—like my work, my writing, my dreams and goals—needed to be off the table. It's possible that she wasn't capable of giving me what I needed. I also couldn't give her what she needed because I felt she didn't know what that was and she didn't yet have the language to tell me. I had to respect that this was her work to do. This letting go of expectations around my mother was a big one, but the weight that fell away was noticeable... immediately.

With the expectation of limitless conversation and connection removed, we started to organically communicate in less pressured ways, like a random text with an Instagram link to a funny reel. It allowed both of us to laugh from across the street. It opened the door for fuller conversation *if* it was something we both needed in the moment. There was no forcing things here. But I knew that, in the meantime, I would have to figure out how to make up for this ~~deficit~~ shift. I needed to find a more fiery connection elsewhere.

Although there's still work to be done, in the summer cycle, I finally released the dream of having a traditional mother-daughter relationship. And I was okay with that. It was a dream that was never really mine. It was a dream I was forcing on myself because I didn't yet have any of the tools I have now, the ones I am offering my community in this book.

It's summer and the leaves are lush and green and there's a sweet scent hovering in the air. I feel a stronger desire to be outside and connect with other people in the summer. When we think about joy and self-love, it's easy enough to assume that we have to surround ourselves with our blood, our immediate family, the people who are supposed to be closest to us. It's human nature to need to be loved, to belong. In her CNN article on the importance of belonging, Amanda Enayati states, "Because as humans, we need to belong. To one another, to our friends and families, to our culture and country, to our world. Belonging is primal, fundamental to our sense of happiness and well-being."[5] But what if the puzzle pieces were shaped in such a way that they could never interlock? We assume a perfect fit is what gives us that feeling of belonging. But what if each family member doesn't magically fit with the others without trying to jam or press them together with a force that is almost painful? We should never bend the edges, right?

How do we connect to the narrative that Black joy is loud and that it's only fully experienced in large groups of family and friends when our own experiences are so far from that? I'm *almost* ready to explore this. But I recognize I need to wait until the end of summer. Because of the heavy letting go I've already done so far, and from seeing how integral slowing down is, I can't rush. I trust myself enough now to lean into creating my own pace for this work.

I had never *asked* my mother what it was she needed to fully love herself. I know this. When I hung up the phone with my friend that day, I felt heard, seen, and understood, but I was also terrified at the notion that there was some blisteringly emotional work to do and I wasn't sure that I had all the right tools I needed to do it. At least not yet. I needed to have conversations with even more Black leaders to continue to grow this toolbox that I'm calling on at the start of every season. Non-negotiables, bringing back joyful activities, affirmations, adjusting my language, saying no with love—these tools are helping to harvest a bounty. Saying no with love comes when you assess whether or not an opportunity or change will give you energy, allow you to show up as your most authentic self, and fit into your current priorities (priorities that should be shifting every year). If it doesn't, you say no with love. In saying no with love, your no is more intentional. Your no is more than just a no, and your response will depend on you. Your no might be concise—"No, this is not a fit"—or it might be "I can't prioritize this right now." Saying no with love can also be connected to changing the relationships with those closest to you. Although I'm not yet ready to have this conversation with my mother, it's in our future.

In trying to explain my own sense of belonging with this close friend, we found it with each other. A lump rose in my throat at the realization that I *could* feel intense love and belonging in my chosen family too. This is where the intense connections lived. I still had work to do, but I felt a small release.

Breathe.

I explore letting go in my novel, *Junie*. As my main character Junie grows into herself, as she intentionally builds her own language for love, her mother moves in the opposite direction. She crumples. Junie knows she cannot stop her. She cannot warn her. But she can show herself love and catch sight of the ripples (and maybe even hope they reach her mother). We don't see a happy ending, for Junie's mother or their relationship. We likely can't even glean it. But sometimes, that's how these relationships go when the patterns of loving that we've watched play out in our daily lives for years and years need to be broken. I intentionally broke this pattern when I decided that the love I have for my mother would need to be shown to her in less overt ways. As I got older, and life's experiences made their way into my marrow, I felt more comfortable with this direction. I hope she does too.

How we show love can vary. I think back to my grandmother with her hands in the dough, to my own mother gathering ingredients and cooking for love, and to me writing letters to myself and showing up for myself, first. Love can be as simple or complex as we make it. *What are some moments of living and loving that you want to stop and acknowledge?*

Looking out my large window at Bear Mountain's waistline and the ombre shades of green shimmying toward me through the shifting wind, I noticed on my windowsill a jar filled with tiny pieces of paper that hold activities that bring me joy: Read a poem out loud. Mindfully drink water. Take a ten-minute stretch. Breathe fully with your eyes closed. Whatever piece of paper I pulled from that jar and whichever activity I fell into, I released a bit of old pain, trapped emotion. I ~~crawled~~ climbed one step forward, and the pattern of unloving that I so willingly followed my whole life slowly started to change direction.

7

~~Pull up~~
<u>Harvest</u> Joy from the Roots

Summer's free-spirited heat still kissed my eyelids as I dreamed about the predictability of fall peering its little head around the corner. But I didn't want to skip ahead and lose sight of the deliciousness of the last, sweetest part of summer. You know, that part where you know you want to exit the season with a bang! I wanted to spend my last piece of summer discovering my joy to date and really listening. Let's map our joy-discovery.

Looking intimately at my own joy-discovery feels like the perfect goal for summer. This book is the first time I have explored my own joy, addressed it formally, and asked questions about it. *Can summer be this for you?* We aren't all "out there" when the sun is closest to us, but *I invite you to consider how certain pieces of yourself take centre stage depending on the season.* My guides also remind me to have realistic expectations too.

Discovering joy can come through failure and by looking back at past decisions through a more experienced lens. Can we find joy inside of past mistakes? Wisdom comes from experiences and living, but it also comes from pain. I remember scrolling through Instagram and stopping on a post that resonated with me: "If you want to know how someone came to know so much, ask them what they've been through." And I just felt so much clarity inside of that. I felt validated. My experiences have value. Living my life as I have is a kind of success.

Like love and joy, success, to me, looks like being ensconced in safety and certainty, and consistently meeting my most basic needs. Success looks like me moving through the world while enriching my communities with every step along the path, as best I can. It looks like ... ease. And ease means existing inside of my full self—a self that continues to evolve—and showcasing that self while being valued for what I bring to the table, no matter whose table it is. A self that speaks up for herself, without apology.

It's natural to question the attainability of ease. It's okay to feel like it is within reach, and then, like a light switch has flicked, you find yourself fumbling in the dark. But since I've been taking this journey with all of you, I sense that a joyous and peaceful way of moving is within arm's reach. This is a reminder that the pathway to successful existence involves sharing difficult experiences in hopes that the ripples reach those who need to hear those stories—and at just the right time. Success is rooted in collective unlearning, even though our experiences and paths will be uniquely different. Sometimes the things we are most afraid to share are the very things that are the most helpful. To carve our own unique path to joy or to redefine and reimagine it, we will have to take small steps into our own experiences. But the point I want to remind myself of is that I can't stay inside my experiences too long and my guides will be the exit plan. When I look back and compare how long I previously allowed myself to sit inside of negative situations to how I act now, the time spent in those emotions has shrunk. This is tracking growth.

I was recently part of a virtual professional publishing panel where I was the only woman on a panel of majority cis white men. After taking my usual time to debrief and write reflectively about my experience immediately post-event—a ritual I built for myself to celebrate and honour the fact that I am indeed a slow processor whose feelings and emotions often arise after the fact—I came to realize that the event was definitely not a space I wanted to be in, and I should have declined the initial invite. But it was too late. Mistakes need to happen on this journey too, though. With every experience, new or old, there's always a ripple to send out, even when we don't know where it will go or who it will touch. A reverberation is meant to come back as a reminder or new learning, and this is what I want to focus on as I walk through this past moment.

Prior to the event, I had prepared pages upon pages of notes, resources, links, and other tools to share with the folks in the room. I dug into my archives and case studies, pulled recommended articles and books to share, and even had some templates to give the audience. And with fall around the corner, it just felt so on brand for me to be in preparation mode.

Within the first ten minutes of the event, it was evident that I was not going to be offered full space to share my expertise. The other panellists were talking over each other and going into long-winded, detailed explanations, whereas I had planned to be clear and concise to allow space for everyone. I continued to wave my virtual hand because as the event progressed, none of the questions were posed to me *first*. I was offered the tail-end scraps of conversations. The men in the room held the space and pushed me onto the sidelines, while I sat waiting for a signal or a breath I could piggyback on. This was not the self that I'd come to know. Many virtual audience members had specific questions for *me*, and I noticed they began to type those queries into the chat. I began to answer those questions in the chat as a last-ditch attempt to be heard. It's the moderator's job to notice this and redirect the conversation. It's the moderator's job to curate the conversation. It's an art.

I want to exit out of that hurt right now. Here is where I want to document growth. Instead of letting anger rise for too long, I used my tools, especially the affirmations, language adjustment, and my guides. I told myself, *You are the master of your own experiences.* I asked myself, *How can I create a resource for my community built from this experience?* A few weeks later, I decided to work on a blog post for my *Nourishing Word* blog that organizers could hopefully use as a tool on how to safely moderate events. It was a very small offering, but I believe this is how real change starts. It must be born from a desire to be part of the change and to come to the table with solution-based movements and suggestions, versus just anger. This is one of the methods I've found myself relying on often: just finding a way to kickstart a solution. It's natural to desire a safe space to share our expertise and ideas. The publishing world offers us little-to-no promises, and we know this going in, so the work we do as individuals, and for ourselves, becomes so important. Our community conversations (or what I like to call living and loving) can help us figure out how to troubleshoot and use our superpowers for good.

Does my joy attach itself to success? Well, in my experience as a Black woman who is excited and eager to share and celebrate things I've overcome, I do feel like we are either not success-ful enough or we are too successful, and then that success is suspect . . . But I think Black people should get the props they deserve for hard work, creativity, perseverance, and sheer determination. I see plenty of successful Black influencers and content creators building empires for themselves, in spaces like TikTok for example. But like the incidents of white folks with platforms taking credit for certain viral dances without citing the source, described by Angelica Tejada in *The Ticker*, "Black talent is used for profit by the privileged."[6]

But we have control over how we uplift and celebrate *each other*. I have a fantastic card on my desk from a good friend that says, "Real friends don't compete, they lift." I look at it daily. I make sure it holds space. I try to make a habit of citing, even verbally, where an idea came from and how I was inspired by it, or I just find ways to pull up and highlight folks doing solid work. I'm not waiting around for the world to celebrate me or my community. If they do, then it's just extra.

Let's take a moment to slow down and acknowledge the air around us right now. We've just done a whole bunch of releasing; together, we let go of narratives that tell us that looking back is negative, that happiness has to start at the beginning of something, that we have to love our bodies all the time, and that we don't deserve second chances. We've worked so hard to let that all go. There's space now to intentionally bring in *more* pockets of joy. Every day of my busy, scheduled life, I try to think of something to look forward to at the end of my work day, whether it's roller skating in my kitchen or lying on the grass and letting the sun's heat tickle my lids. I *try* to ~~schedule~~ be a magnet for joy.

Joy isn't always accessible. It doesn't just show up. I have to admit that, although I've let go, I thought I'd feel a lot lighter at this point in the season, so there's obviously still work to do. I guess I haven't done all the releasing that I needed to. *Check in with yourself too. How are you feeling?* There are still things tied to my heart, and the recent event experience I described can account for more of the weight.

What am I carrying forward in this season, and how can I make the space for it? Let me document this.

When I think back to that event and how I felt the pressure of having to de-centre my own Blackness and expertise, and how we as a community are expected to show up in white spaces, I can't help but return to body talk. I think about what Ian Williams says in "Swimming," the first piece in his book *Disorientation*. He uses the metaphor of swimming and interrogates the stereotype that "Black people can't swim" to talk about his own experience with racism and how he, inside of his own Black body, is still today discovering how to put his own feet in the water. "In water, we each look a little different because we are both affected by the same element. The journey out of ignorance takes us into—forgive the mushy term—self-discovery and into a more consuming empathetic relation to the prevailing issues of our time."[7] None of this comes without the simple act of slowing down.

What is it about the Black body that intimidates? You know I hear Maya Angelou's poem "Still I Rise" in my head when I ask that question, right? Ha ha! Ahhh, yes. I feel like I need to call on my Black writers right now. When things get murky, I find myself relying on my guides more and more.

I recover my joy at this moment. This time, it feels effortless.

Yes! It's always my Black writers who call me back in, remind me of the joy within reach and how I need to fight to make sure 1) I don't forget its position, where it sits, the pockets it resides in, and 2) I remember how powerful I am as a Black woman and how my community can benefit when we create our own methodology of happiness. This is the sisterhood I need to rally when I feel weighed down, hopeless even. I may have to spend every single part of my day buried in the dirt, doing my share of the joy-discovery, but no one can take my Black women writers away from me. Just like the images and words permanently inked under my skin, no one can take them away.

That is *my* truth, y'all. Mmm.

How can we celebrate our accomplishments to their fullest? I am reminded of an incredible event I hosted with two other fabulous Black women writers. I decided that, yes, I can have some control over how I celebrate and that I didn't necessarily have to wait around for permission. For an hour, the incredibly talented, multi-disciplinary Wanda Taylor and the doula, writer, and book coach Danielle Jernigan joined me on Zoom to talk about all the amazing things we had on the go, and we laughed, we lifted each other up, and we just had fun. No agenda, no "key takeaways"; just heart and soul in a space that we created. I definitely want more of that. There is a lot I can do (and a lot you can do too) to create moments of celebration. We can be powerful in the way we share space and uplift each other, and just be in the moment.

It was then and there that I decided to continue to have control over the spaces I put my body in. I wanted to make informed decisions about my body. I wanted to understand why certain things were happening to me or failing me. To do this, I had to relearn my body. I could give myself that.

My continuing failures are how I continue to rise. Due to some body complications and unsatisfactory experiences with medical specialists, I decided to go the holistic route and enlisted a naturopath. With that choice, I felt something shift.

They say knowledge is power, and they weren't kidding! Wisdom and knowledge can stem from pain. I watched myself ask questions with confidence, and I held onto the information offered because of how detailed and accessible it was. This felt right. I learned more about my body in that one-hour appointment with the naturopath than I had in years. I took things one step further and signed up for menstrual coach Natalie Martin's Love Your Flow course, where I learned so much about how the changes in my cycle were telling me something was wrong. As a Black female coach with mindfulness and care clearly prioritized in her business, Martin centres her teachings on the importance of body literacy and rest. I discovered joy in the most unexpected of places—inside the small failures of my body. My entire body relaxed. My body was communicating and, for the first time, I was listening.

8

~~On Introversion~~
Embrace the Art of
Deep Listening

"I find a lot of healing from being alone."
—Kenitra Dominguez, in conversation with the author, 2021

D oes anyone else grieve near the end of summer? When we think about the other seasons (winter especially), we eagerly count the days for them to disappear. But the end of summer feels like a loss of freedom. Summer holds so many opportunities to push everything into the background, be present, and just listen to what the world is trying to say.

It's difficult for me to even come close to describing the joy that comes from being listened to. And I don't mean someone *hearing* me, I mean being completely listened to. You know, the kind of listening where all the outward distractions blur and you are holding the complete attention of someone who is waiting to be surprised.

We live in a fast-paced world where people listen to respond or react, versus listening to understand. As someone with an introverted personality, it often takes me a bit longer to get my thoughts in order and then more time to process them. But most people are impatient and interrupt. And this is either because my mindful pause has led the other person to think that I've finished, or they just couldn't be bothered to wait for me to complete my thought. This can be so frustrating. In certain spaces, I have found it easier to just sit in silence. But I want to unlearn this, because sitting in silence does not align with who I am or who I am becoming. In fact, silence as a response is something I want to let go of.

Taking a moment here to big myself up: I have a lot of gorgeous things to say, but in order for everything to come out and land the way I want it to, it requires the right listener, a safe space, and time.

I recently had an incredible conversation with singer-songwriter Shakura S'Aida about my previous book, *Junie*, for a live audience, and we talked about safety and space. Before we took the virtual stage, we had a conversation to get to know one another. This too was an act of slowing down.

During the event, I was in awe of myself. I sat in front of my large painting of Toni Morrison, and of course that was the first thing she noticed when our cameras flicked on. I naturally called on my literary guides as I was speaking to her, and then, for the first time, they slipped away. It was as if they could tell I was safe with Shakura. It was as if it were only her and me in the room. The audience melted away too. Shakura's natural ability to listen felt like being held, cradled. I could say and *be* anything in that space and no harm would come to me, but oddly enough, I only wanted to be myself. Before we even stepped on stage together, she told me, "I want to keep you safe." I'll never forget that. What an offering from one Black woman to another. *I want to keep you safe.* No one has ever said that to me before, and it affected me more than I'll be able to describe. But I can't fail if I try.

The next day, I was out walking my dog and the sun was out after a week-long bout of pelting rain. I stopped with Bear Mountain behind me, and the first edges of the morning sun flickered across the back of my neck. I had my headphones on, and I stood there, for how long I can't recall. But a song called "So Big" by Musiq Soulchild and Syleena Johnson started to play. I stood there with my eyes closed, and without any push-back or resistance, I let myself cry. I felt not only an extreme burst of gratitude for having been in such a space the night before, but also like the song was a love letter to myself. The words and lyrics felt like the words I would sing now to my younger self. I would keep her safe. I would *sing* to her.

As a slow processor, the way I genuinely experienced the event with Shakura took fourteen hours to show itself. But when it came, it was an experience I'll not soon forget. *Friends, can you think of a time where you felt like that just from a conversation? Take a minute now and breathe that out.* To me, this is what deep listening can do. Deep listening can smooth out all the wrinkles life left on you—even if only temporarily. Deep listening can remind you that there are so many tiny shim-mery moments of joy tucked under painful things. Friends, we deserve the space to hold these small moments. This is the space I try to create for everyone in my world because I've been witness to the ripples that flow from this act. To have it reciprocated changed me forever.

What if my introversion elevated my ability to listen and be listened to? What if I was someone who listened so intently, patiently, with an engaged body language? What if others have experienced the safety that I felt with Shakura?

When I was young, I was always made to feel that there was something wrong with being quiet, and I used to believe it was connected to me being a girl. I think back to my older brother, who perhaps wasn't considered quiet, but he wasn't overly boisterous either. So why was I the one absorbing all the neg-ative vibes because of my reservedness? People were always whispering around me, "Oh she's so *shy*, isn't she? Honey, that girl doesn't say much, does she?"

In an article about parenting introverted children on the Quiet Revolution website, Jennifer Granneman shares, "Many introverts–children and adults–struggle with feeling 'heard' by others."[8] She goes on to quote Dr. Marti Olsen Laney's book *The Hidden Gifts of the Introverted Child*, where it's stated that introverts "live internally, and they need someone to draw them out," and "without a parent who listens and reflects back to them, like an echo, what they are thinking, they can get lost in their own minds."[9] I did not yet know this was my super-power and where my gift might take me.

I can confirm this would have been a helpful tool for my family in "assessing" me instead of making me retreat further into myself. But I think they simply didn't know what they didn't know, so I don't blame them, because I too had no clue until this moment that my introversion was connected to my ability to listen and my desire to be listened to. And even though difficult relationships with family and even some friends have left cracks in my foundation, the summer has me thinking: If I had the ability to run my hand along that crack now, would I be able to feel hope pushing through the raised scar pulsing underneath my fingertips? If I slowed down long enough to listen to it, could I experience again and again that same burst of exceptional gratitude that I felt with Shakura? On this quest to joy and self-love, I am happy to say I can see the other side of that wound. There's a vast horizon there.

I'm not afraid to admit that since childhood, I've spent the next eighty seasons trying to change myself. And friends, trying to be someone you are not is hard work. It's exhausting. And it's not worth it. I'll tell you that much. And now that I am diving into this, I can't help but wonder if my past toxic friendships and romantic relationships happened over and over because of this extreme desire to climb out of what I can now name as my deep-listening superpower.

Being an introvert can be much more nuanced and intricate than being shy. And in fact, in that same article on introversion, Jennifer Granneman writes that labelling a child as shy can be harmful. "'Shy' is a word that carries a negative connotation. If your introverted child hears the word 'shy' enough times, she may start to believe that her discomfort around people is a fixed trait, not a feeling she can learn to control." She goes on to say that "'Shy' focuses on the inhibition she experiences, and it doesn't help her understand the true source of her quietness—her introverted temperament."

I chose to speak with Kenitra Dominguez, an American career coach for Black and WOC introverts, because of the way I felt seen and heard when I stumbled upon her Instagram page. This was probably the first time I saw another Black woman entrepreneur openly talking about being an introvert. What?! So this is a thing? Okay, I was definitely listening now. I followed her posts and hopped into her Instagram live sessions.

When we chatted on Zoom, I felt an immediate connection, which is hard enough to do on Zoom, let alone for two introverts! When speaking about the workplace and how we as Black female introverts fit in, it was incredible to listen to our stories blend and morph into one very familiar experience. I spoke about breaking the nine-to-five work template and how I wanted to build something bigger than myself. Kenitra held me. She listened. We didn't interrupt each other. At the time I didn't realize that this entrepreneurial passion was actually pushing me into self-love because I was resisting all the things, spaces, and obligations that drained me or took too much from me. And as an entrepreneur herself, Kenitra just got it. She also felt more empowered as an entrepreneur than she has in her previous life.

Like me, she values autonomy over her life, which has allowed her to take better care of herself, emotionally, mentally, and when working remotely, where she can avoid the prying eyes of her co-workers. We have the space to just be us, authentically. Entrepreneurship is often a solution for the Black female introvert. Wait: language adjustment (hello, summer tools). From here on out, I'm replacing the word *introvert* with *deep listener*. Y'all ready for our empires or what?

Kenitra uses her ~~introversion~~—oops, <u>deep-listening skills</u>—and entrepreneurial mindset to organically replenish and self-nourish. When she mentioned that her husband was away for the weekend, we both threw our heads back and laughed at the same time. We both thought the same thing: we get energy from being alone because it's an opportunity to fully listen to ourselves, our ideas, and our dreams. We both felt like we could experience the same explosive feeling of gratitude from being alone, just as we could experience it here together. It doesn't mean that we can't share space with select people, but getting breaks from the pressure of sharing space is always a welcomed gift. I'm pinning this new learning right on top of my learning from Shakura. Oooh, I'm going to have to let go of a few things to make more space! Good thing summer is almost ending and the unlearning is coming.

As ~~introverts~~ deep listeners, we take in our environments all at once. We are like birds flying above. We see it all. This can be both beautiful and overwhelming. I think back to the many times I was out at a restaurant, maybe a work gathering of my colleagues, and I could hear each and every conversation all at once—and how I felt this incredible desire to escape. It wasn't because I was anti-social, it was because my environment was screaming in my ear and I couldn't do what I do best, which is listen intently to one person at a time.

As ~~introverts~~ deep listeners we find holistic connections inside of our own heads. Inner thought becomes intellectual conversation. It also means that we pay close attention when having real-life conversations and the expectations are high. It will take a lot of work to get to know ~~an introvert~~ a deep listener because they will not just regurgitate everything about themselves in one go. It has to be earned over the course of many years. I remember meeting a few extroverted friends back in the day and the overwhelming feeling of their monologue-like life dump! How does ~~an introverted person~~ a deep listener match that? When I first met my current partner and before we got together, I would walk around him in silence. I never initiated conversation. I just listened. I paid attention. Years later, while we unpacked the boxes in our new home, he shared, "I remember when I first met you, you never said a word to me. Now you're never quiet." I smile at the thought. At the memory. It's so true to who I am. Maybe that particular comment would have embarrassed me before or been a cause for defensiveness. Not now. Now it feels like a part of my DNA that I proudly wear. A cape I never want to remove.

I spoke with entrepreneur Terrance Lee, author of the book *Quiet Voice Fearless Leader* and a self-proclaimed engineer-turned-introvert-leader, about how, through research into his introversion, his silence also became his superpower. Terrance wanted to figure out when he started to become ~~an introvert~~ a deep listener because, unlike me, he was social as a kid. So the question then became, when did this change? In his book, he explores an experience from his youth when a choir teacher called him out publicly in front of his peers. Terrance thinks his introversion started there. During our conversation, he says "So many people have things that happen to them when they are young, but we don't realize the impact." This is true. I think back to my many interactions with family when I was young. Heck, they even spoke about me while I was in the same room! That feeling of invisibility (although a superpower in some narratives) wasn't cool for me as the future change-maker who needed and wanted to be seen.

When I asked Terrance what deep listening looked like to him, he said, "I want to think before I respond. A lot of people just shoot from the hip. They say the first thing that comes to their mind. Deep listening is not listening to hear but listening to understand. Most just listen to respond, already ready to go in with their response, but it's unfortunate because when we do that, we are discounting another person's truth." Word!

Oddly enough, I've found that being around extroverts is the best way to avoid the pressure to be the life of the party or the centre of attention. But I can tell that in the past, family, friends, and folks in my own professional circles thought the quiet behaviour to be suspect. And back then, I didn't have the language I have now—thank you, summer tools—to properly assess and speak back against the gaslighting attached to these kinds of unspoken criticisms. And at seven years old, I *definitely* didn't know what ~~an introvert~~ a deep listener was—or that wider society would misunderstand what ~~an introvert~~ a deep listener was—nor could I predict how this would allow me to lead spaces with extreme confidence and clarity. My ~~introversion~~ deep listening has always *been* a superpower, I just didn't know how to use it.

In her 2021 article about not being social at work, Brianna Holt writes about Tia Burroughs's response to one of her tweets about Black women not being allowed to be ~~introverts~~, or what I am now dubbing <u>deep listeners</u>: "She blames the negative stereotypes associated with Black women, like angry, mean, and aggressive, as the cause for this unfeasible standard to be hypersocial and accommodating in White spaces, while White people simply get to be themselves."[10] I can't say I connected to this until now, because I think there's more to it than this. Even though this statement is accurate, does it mean that we can't have control over the spaces we choose to be in? When I was initially asked to do the event with Shakura S'Aida, I slowed down (thank you, spring tools) and I asked myself, What do I need in order to show up as my best self? It was then that I *requested* to work with Shakura. I *requested* a virtual space. I *requested* my own safety. I saw how differently I showed up. Looking back, I can admit that the event was my first time showing up as my whole authentic self, as I was becoming her. If nothing else, we have control over how we show up.

I want to show all the unique sides of me and all the possibilities connected to how my joy may very well be different from anyone else's joy, but that it is mine nonetheless. We all carve out our own paths. We all, no matter our background, history, experiences, family upbringing, or place of birth, deserve happiness as defined by us. Sometimes we will need to rewrite the narrative written on our behalf and bask in the heat of the summer's drift into fall.

Like Brianna Holt, I believe that we should normalize personality traits that showcase the variety of ways in which we can show up as our true selves. When I get asked to do a "sensitivity" read of the Black female character in a white writer's project, I often say yes for this reason. If I have the opportunity to change the ways in which Black women are portrayed in pop culture and literature, I'm going to jump at the opportunity, because, like Téa said, this is a second chance at living.

I want you to think about and focus on what the unlearning has laid out for you so far, because this is just the start of this work. For me, the biggest, most luscious epiphany so far came from my overarching goal of slowing down. Slowing down has also prepared me for the work to come this fall and winter—the hard work that we have to do despite the weather. Because of my desire for time with the self, I uncovered my new ~~introversion~~ deep-listening superpower. And this is what has created the most light on this journey. When I looked back at all the language adjustments I made, I felt more powerful, more in control. It helped see into the future, and the seasons ahead are going to be vital, I just sense it.

I am learning more than I had expected to, but it's the unlearnings I want to say are the most powerful. The load lightens every time I drop something off and just let it go.

So here we are at the end of summer's heat, our bodies glistening and also tired from a season of gathering, showcasing, and connecting. It's always a bit sad to see the summer end. There's a specific shift in energy, almost like someone shuts off the lights.

Do you want to celebrate for a minute? I know now that my being quiet was just me listening intently. It was me preparing myself for all the incredible things I wanted to do in the world. *Is there anything language-related that you can change?* Thanks to the backside of summer, I have sharpened my listening skills for another season. Now that I have recognized this knowledge, no more hiding or trying to change it. Pivotal moment, no turning back. No more holding on to things that do not serve me. So what does my ability to listen look like when the ground has been watered, seeds planted, and sun shining?

—

Summer *Un*learnings

LET'S UNLEARN:
SISTERHOOD AS A SINGULAR EXPERIENCE.

Just like there is no one Black experience, there shouldn't be any one clear definition of sisterhood either. I can build a community for close relationships where the nurturing is reciprocal and not adversarial or competitive. I can ask for the other deep listening Black girls. I can make room for my past literary guides, and there is power in knowing this. I also don't have to force relationships because society tells me "this is what sisterhood is," and that it's all I have. I'll decide that, thank you very much.

LET'S UNLEARN:
FAMILIAL LOVE IS UNCONDITIONAL.

I've always disliked that phrase "blood is thicker than water," so I'm gonna go ahead and let that go. Chosen family is a big conversation these days. This doesn't have to mean that blood families have to be pushed out of the ring; it simply means that I can dictate the closeness of these relationships and that sometimes loving from across the street is how we nourish fragile relationships. I think this one is going to take a few cycles to really thicken, but the work has started and I gotta acknowledge that. It counts. It's a step forward.

LET'S UNLEARN: HAPPINESS CAN'T EXIST INSIDE OF TUMULTUOUS TIMES.

I remember feeling guilty for laughing during rough patches in my life or feeling shame for taking care of myself when the world felt like it was crumbling. I even felt guilty for visibly resting. The world will always be crumbling, and we shouldn't have to wait for some non-existent fairy tale to show itself before we can crack a smile or just do the small things that bring us a moment of happiness. Isn't life made up of these small moments? I'll collect as many as I can!

LET'S UNLEARN: BEING LOUD = BEING HEARD.

I will always demand the presence of the folks who are willing to pay close attention to the whispers in the back. Being loud doesn't mean anything, y'all. Divulging everything about yourself all at once just means there is nothing else to get to uncover. Anyone who chooses to get to know me will not have to relearn me every season, but they will come into my past slowly, over years. That's a big commitment, and you better believe I pay attention to those who make it.

LANGUAGE ADJUSTMENTS

~~introvert~~ <u>deep listeners</u>
~~cut folks out~~ <u>revisit loving ways to let go</u>
~~suffocating~~ <u>overstimulating</u>
~~hold us back~~ <u>stall our growth</u>
~~crawled~~ <u>climbed</u>
~~schedule~~ <u>be a magnet for joy</u>

Pay attention to your own language as you move forward. Do this by listening to the words you use every day. Take your time. Choose different words even after you've said them. This is another way of going back. What are you nervous about? What are you ready for? Slowing down allows you to be proactive and provides more opportunities for clarity and ease.

Don't forget to revisit the cyclical questions from the community call to carry you forward:

- What do I need or want to make space for right now?

- How am I really feeling? I want to be honest about my feelings with myself and others.
- What feels heavy? I want to try to let go of this by season's end.

"Turn your wounds into wisdom."

—Oprah Winfrey

Fall Community Call:

Establishing Non-negotiables

Nature is at its most vibrant in the fall and it can provide us a sense of creativity and liminality. It can be unnerving and tranquil at the same time. Nature can cause us to mix our metaphors too. There is so much happening in nature during the fall season as colours shift and textures shift and dry out—it can be confusing. But this is exactly why we need to set boundaries in the fall. This will be my favourite chunk of work yet. My tools for this season's work will include aligning my priorities and establishing non-negotiables.

Another tool I'll be leaning on is creating methods for slowing down now that I know how integral it is to my joy. The unlearning I know I want to achieve by season's end will include testing some big belief systems.

By this point, I think it will be obvious to me (and hopefully to you too) how different our journeys have been. We should celebrate that too. This is what we've been trying to do since the beginning of the book.

REMINDER

As the seasons continue to shift, so do we. Let's look back so that we can pivot and remap our journeys into a healthier sense of self. Let's sit inside of our own identity.

LET'S FOCUS

At the beginning of each season, I call on all of you to ask yourselves the same three questions:

- What do I need or want to make space for right now?
- How am I really feeling? I want to be honest about my feelings with myself and others.
- What feels heavy? I want to try to let go of this by season's end.

9

I Will Build a Sense of Self

"Self-love is not urgent."
—Meghan Watson, in conversation with the author, 2021

When I hear the word *boundary* now, I get excited. This wasn't always the case. The word itself used to feel abrasive, like someone was rubbing sandpaper all over my body. Changing my relationship with the word and using it as one of my fall tools is what opened the door to building a comfortable relationship with boundary work. This was only one small step, though. So I'll go ahead and call on y'all to be open to this small step and *see if you can come up with at least one new boundary to commit to putting into action by the end of this fall season.* Don't worry, it's okay if we all move at different paces. Planning the work we need to do is urgent, but self-love itself can't be.

The more I slow down, the more I am called into appreciating all the old selves I've gotten to know over the past few cycles. I wouldn't want to erase those selves, but I do want them to feel purposeful. Friends, it's true, my insides *have* been burned by the heat of trauma, and my past experiences have informed my movements, actions, decisions, and even mistakes of today, but I feel a bit closer to saying that those moments don't define me. Because of those conversations with the Black leaders and my hard work, I can now slowly begin to separate my past experiences from the version of me today. *So go ahead and take a moment to sit with this idea. What have you come into so far? Remember those soft intentions you set when I first introduced you to our guides? How are you doing?* I don't think I would have had the tools and confidence to even check in with you about this in this process had I not spent so much time talking about joy and self-love with other Black folks. So you know what? I am proud of myself.

Where do you find your strength? Think about your own tools and guides. Go ahead and take a little gratitude moment, y'all. Let me breathe that in too.

Let's go inward. And I mean, *really* inward. We cannot learn to love ourselves and pull joy from it without understanding ourselves within the context of our environment. I don't mean just our socio-political environment but our natural environment and how much we mean to the world and the world means to us. Tell me this isn't the perfect work to do in fall! At this point, the seasons continue to act as my trusted guide through this often-tumultuous work of self-realignment. Fall makes me pay attention to change, and it gives me the biggest, most simple signal: put away the shorts and pull on your boots and scarves. And not only is the season throwing out signals, but our ever-changing world is showing us how it impacts other living creatures. With my slowing down, I've been able to see this more closely. With my own unique relationship with the natural world beginning to open up, I find myself curious about how our movements in the world can change the lives of the animals that also seek out safety and community. When I walked down the trails behind my home in fall, I'd often see squirrels scurrying with acorns in their mouths, moving from this tree to that. They were planning. They knew what they needed for winter and they were getting ready. In which ways do their lives mirror ours?

One of my favourite parts of autumn is the way the leaves drift slowly from their branches. I can't help but to stop where I stand, look up and notice how they detach themselves from a previous self that no longer serves them. They let themselves go. To me, that releasing is intentional and powerful. They are stepping aside to create a space for a new self to step in. Contrary to what we might think, moving away from older selves is not a naive way to avoid the pain of the past season, it's quite the opposite. It's a way for the leaves to say I am done living inside of this outdated self, and in order to make space for a new version, I must let these layers dust the ground so that the new buds can take on these new experiences. I must let go. I must let this past be crunched under the soles of passersby. In other words, when thinking about building up and paying close attention to this sense of self, I had to speak loudly to the old versions of self and embolden them to fall and crumble like ash at my feet. Fall is a guide, but it's also a witness.

Self-love is letting go, but it is also grieving. Can we mourn an old version of ourselves even if it was a problematic layer? Can we forgive ourselves for the times when we didn't know how to respond? Once we've let go of parts of ourselves that had to go, we need to walk toward that new self. That old self was a bridge that helped us arrive at this new space—a bridge we needed to walk over in order to get here. I have to think about this, visualize it, when days are tough or barriers upon barriers are placed in front of me. I know there is a bigger purpose to it. That does at least help me take that first step onto the bridge. I know there is still work ahead, even after that first step. We can't cross that bridge and enter a new space without grieving what we left behind. To let go is to pull old belief systems up from the ground. Uproot them. But there is so much fear in this uprooting. Sometimes it can be difficult to let go of ourselves because we've never fully learned to exist *within* ourselves. It was bell hooks who said, "Knowing how to be solitary is central to the art of loving. When we can be alone, we can be with others without using them as a means of escape."[1] Then being with ourselves becomes a balm. It's the very start of belonging. But then why is most of society so dead set on being surrounded by people? Maybe we haven't learned to be alone yet because we are too focused on trying to fit in.

Belonging is not automatic. And it can mean different things to different people. Now that I let myself play with my language, let's sort out what belonging means to us as individuals.

I remember the very first time I took a writing class and stepped into the workshop room. It was late in the season, I felt the chill in my fingertips from the hour-plus journey on public transit to get there. The room was small but lustrous, and there were others already in the room, casually flinging their jackets and scarves over the backs of their chairs. They were smiling and chuckling like they already shared some common bond. I can't recall a time where I felt more nervous. I spent most of the two-hour class looking down at my paper, keeping all my ideas to myself, locked inside like a hurricane whipping to get out. But looking back at that day more than a decade ago, I can break the experience down to its parts and see that I was expecting a feeling of immediate connection. I wasn't prepared to feel inexperienced, in competition, or even protective of my words and how I got them down on the page. I was expecting to belong, immediately, based on some outside expectation of what belonging really was. Time to redefine that some more for myself.

At this point, I've reached an opportunity to relearn myself and run my hands down my scars while celebrating all the parts of me I never paid attention to, or the parts I felt weren't worthy of attention. Like in the fall, we can exist in two phases at the same time. This work can be breathtakingly sumptuous and terrifying all at once. And this is where my boundary work comes in. How can I protect the fragile parts of myself while I am in repair mode? In speaking with other Black folks about their own relationships to the innermost parts of themselves, it brought me closer to letting go of my frayed layers and closer to loving the scars that remain. I can love the parts that I don't need to let go of. This is both invigorating and difficult. I am forty years old, and only recently have I investigated a sense of self. For a moment, I felt guilty about showing up "so late" to do this work. I also worried that friends and family might say, "You've changed." But I now have the tools to exit that ever-present negative self-talk. This doesn't mean that I am immune to the ups and downs that are attached to self-growth, but it means that I no longer stay in the harmful shadow of my own self-doubt for as long. I started by creating a boundary for myself. It has to start with the self. This boundary within myself that I set *for* myself is that I will not allow negative self-talk to live within me. Yes, I will stumble and I will catch myself saying things I don't mean. But this self-boundary acts as a reminder to slow down, rejig, and change my language if I need to. Boundaries are about us, not other people. We build the boundary, communicate the boundary, and stay true to the promised consequences if these boundaries are broken. This is not easy work. I can see the most miniscule bits of growth and feel called to celebrate them regularly. This progress is real, y'all. I no longer think about the transition between who I am and who I am becoming as a quick and clear transition, but instead I look at myself through a blurry lens that, over time, becomes more clear. Journeying through self-love is like slowly wiping the cloth across the cloudy lens over and over.

Self-love is a process. Growing into ourselves is how we can see more clearly. It can be gentle and supportive, but it can also be messy, and because self-love and journeying into unearthing joy has no end point, we can and should love ourselves even when the growth isn't easy to spot.

Having used the summer as an opportunity to let go, and having explored the world of boundary-setting, next I will embark on the work of self-trust. At the beginning of fall, I let go of a lot of self-doubt, which means I can now start the journey into self-trust. Just like reflection and looking back, self-trust plays a huge role in change, letting go. While building a writing workshop on self-trust, I fell upon a *Psychology Today* article by Charlie and Linda Bloom that stated, "The definition of self-trust is the firm reliance on the integrity of yourself. There is a difference between a life that is grounded in self-trust and one that is not. When we look at examples of people who are self-trusting, we find that they have clarity and confidence in their choices."[2] And this is where the boundary work elevated for me. I wanted to feel good about saying no with love and saying yes with conditions. I wanted to be firm in the decisions I made without allowing others to push back.

In a blog post I published on my website, I decided to take some space to write about the first time I said no to a misaligned writing opportunity, and I'll share that story with you here: I felt an indescribable energy move through my body. I was suddenly powerful and in control of my creative realm for the first time. Don't get me wrong, saying no was not immediate or easy and it didn't happen without a lot of preparation, building of methods, and of course, prioritizing. But when I finally hit a ceiling for taking on projects I didn't want, or worse, projects that didn't align, I knew the time had come to create a new, more intentional path for myself. That "no" was just the beginning of a movement. Saying no to that project allowed me to spend time dreaming and plotting the creative life that I wanted for myself—the life where I could choose who I wanted to work with, schedule my days based on energy, build processes and workflows, and automate admin tasks: the creative life that I was told I couldn't have or didn't exist. But I wouldn't be me if I didn't resist the template, push the narrative, and challenge myself as a writer and as an entrepreneur.

Before saying no with love (or saying yes with conditions) I ask myself five questions:

1. Do I really want to say yes to this? If so, why?
2. Does this fit into my current set of priorities?
3. Is this project going to give me energy or take from my energy?
4. Can I set aside the necessary time to complete the project and with a sense of joy?
5. Will this project allow me to show up as my authentic self?

Asking these questions became part of the catalyst for my annual Say No with Love workshop. This workshop uses similar questions as reflective opportunities to explore who we are, what we want, and how we want to show up in our lives.

Through group writing exercises and discussion, this creativity and time-management workshop is meant to help folks uncover vital priorities for the year, unearth their authentic selves, and hopefully lead them to finding balance. Through a unique decision-making process, it helps generate true contentment and satisfaction in their careers and creative practices. In fact, I've started building two guided journals, the first one based on this workshop, because of how popular it has been and how many young creatives have benefitted from it, and the second one connected to creating a time-capsule/ book-promotion tool for debut authors. When we have clear priorities and create ways to simply "touch" these priorities on a daily basis, we can't help but build an intimate relationship with the business side of being a writer.

None of this saying-no-with-love stuff comes without risks. I used to make decisions based solely on money, saying yes to things out of fear that no one will ask again. It's not easy to say no when you are simply trying to make a living as a writer or as a creative in general. But taking on projects that do not align will take *more* from you than what you receive monetarily. This was a difficult lesson for me to learn, but an important one. We all have access to the same twenty-four hours a day, and what you do with it is up to you, but we can control where our energy goes, even in a nine-to-five job where we *think* we have no say. But this is work we can all do, whether you are a creative or not. Remember that you can take on general tools as an entry point to getting started. The specificity comes from your actions and how you apply these tools to your own unique situation.

In 2019 I launched my own business, Breathing Space Creative. In a way, I was entering into a new self, or coming closer to one that was always there. But in order to get here, I had to let go of old versions of myself (the selves that told me that I was not good enough to build something for myself and the selves that believed I should always dim my light) and investigate my language like I did at the end of spring and all through the summer. I had to look closely at old belief systems and possibly even do some letting go there too. My vision for this business was that I would work with writers to help them build and transform their writing processes through the lens of self-defined wellness and self-care. I wanted to help creatives see all the branches on their own trees and embrace the idea that some leaves were supposed to fall. In fact, I wanted them to predict and prepare for that shedding. I wanted them to see how this foundational work on the self poured into their creative lives. I wanted them to see every branch on that tree and how it connected to the trunk, the roots, and soil. I wanted to create a holistic conversation around creative life, productivity, and burnout. I wanted them to see how much control they really had. *When it comes to your own daily lives, where do you have the most control?*

When I was the managing editor at a local literary magazine, I had good intentions, and of course I wanted to be productive. At the time, I had no idea that my own ridiculous definition of "being productive" was not sustainable, but I didn't want to burden my team and ask for additional help. I didn't have the tools yet and I hadn't known I could call on my guides. But looking back, I can recognize that I started to plant seeds for myself. When I left the role at the magazine to start my own business, the first thing I did was ask for help and pay an assistant for five hours of help a month (that's probably what I spent on coffee anyway). And the second thing I did was to sit down and map out what I could realistically do myself. If I couldn't take something on, I needed to find the money to hire help in some way. **Moment to harvest: I need to invest in myself early.**

The word *productive* is now redefined by me as showing up for myself first and doing whatever it is that I need to do in order to put my body's needs ahead of meeting anyone else's needs or deadlines. But to sustain this, we have to slow down. I started a new routine: During the first thirty minutes of my day, I assessed what it was I needed. Water? A stretch? How did I feel? Those first thirty minutes were mine, no matter how much work I had on my plate, and I then prioritized my top three tasks for the day. Everything else could wait. This is the narrative I told myself over and over and over until I started to live it. I slipped up a lot, but because I saw almost immediate results from the boundary of thirty minutes of protection at the start of my day, I needed to help others do the same. It was so simple and such a small step, but if folks took that first step, I knew the results would come trickling in. I bolstered the Say No with Love workshop from this, and I now offer it for free to the public every year. When I am nourished, I can give back to my community. Interesting how that works!

In my business, I work with all creatives, but more specifically I help people transform themselves as writers. I focus the person *inside* the writer by helping them build strong and healthy habits and take care of their minds and bodies while being curious about the world around them. The publishing industry rarely focuses on the storytellers as much as they focus on the stories. But I suppose that's the nature of the industry. It's not due to anyone wanting to ignore the storyteller, they just can't do it all. I wanted to step up and help with this work. I am helping writers to build a sense of self. But I recognize that I express this work outwardly, hardly saving a bite or two for myself. But this year, this season, I am refocusing that and I know now that I need to begin to offer myself the same tools, support, and advice that I so lovingly push into my community of creatives. And most importantly, I want to allow myself the opportunity to fail. I want to dive into what it feels like not to belong. Failure, for me, means not trying. It means stopping yourself out of fear. But failing is an exercise that we all need some experience with.

The first time I launched my author-care program, I couldn't get one publisher to say yes. That feeling of failure was there. I had two options as I saw them: 1) take the no for an answer and not even try to keep moving forward or 2) tuck things away, investigate the resistance, and rebuild. I chose to rebuild. *How can you apply this to your own work?*

Earlier in the year, I wrote a keynote on belonging, and this chapter clarified that work. See, it's serendipitous how slowing down and focusing on similarities instead of differences helps us see all the linking threads and get a glimpse of the bigger picture. When I spoke to registered psychotherapist Meghan Watson, we fell into this beautiful conversation about nature. We discussed how the seasons have not put forth some predictable timeline for us to follow. We put that timeline on nature. But despite the labels we've placed on spring, summer, fall, and winter, the seasons continue to just be. They just exist. They power on the way they always have, and it is this that I think we'll find the biggest message of all. Speaking with Meghan was like speaking to a side of myself that I always wanted to get to know. Our conversation was so aligned; we fed off each other, moved back and forth in ways I'd not thought possible when meeting someone for the first time.

Unlike me, with my seemingly late journey into building a sense of self, everything Meghan Watson does is rooted in self-love. I admire this so much. Whether it's her work as a therapist, her writing, or her exploration of self, love is always the medium. We talked intently about taking time, moving slowly, and not rushing the process of self-love. It was from Meghan that I learned it was okay to stop and acknowledge the world around me. "We can be so blindly walking through

life and numbly walking through the world without paying attention . . . It's a way of *not* loving ourselves. The world
around us can add to this love. This process cannot be rushed."
I have so much gratitude for this learning.

Take a reflective breath in.

Self-love is gentle, supportive. But self-love can also be messy
when we turn inward like this. We have to learn to love how we
show up in the world, even if we can't see the growth yet. That's
the difficult part. But in speaking with Meghan, I realized that
I'm not the only one who thinks about growth in this way. Documenting and celebrating the smallest of steps forward can
have a monumental impact on this journey. As we journey into
the self, we can also pick up seeds along the way and give these
to our community.

But there can be remorse when we don't get it right. We can
be self-critical and unforgiving, but this is what we are here to
work on, right? Fall, for me, is about warm foods in my belly. I
love taking my time to make soups and stews for my family. I
imagine a pot of stew on the stove. I periodically taste it, pulling the spoon to my lips. As disappointment floods my body
because the taste is off or not yet there, I can grieve that failure.
But from Meghan, I learn that I may not have all the ingredients
this season and maybe it will be right later. She told me that
"the artfulness of self-love is a tuning to the emotions you feel

in that process and not using them as weapons against where you want to go." What if I dumped that entire pot of stew in the trash? Stew that could have fed my community with love? I think back to my conversation with Ifrah, too, and I put the spoon back in the pot.

I've been incredibly lucky to be surrounded by so many incredible Black folks. But this joy, like much of what I've experienced, can seem temporary. I've thought about the spaces I've been in where the white gaze was oh so prominent; spaces where I couldn't fully flex, couldn't completely be myself. I craved the inner rooms where I could fling a rant onto the wall at full volume without the whipping around of heads or the tsk-tsking of the white folks in the room. A part of building up and coming into this sense of self means I want to let go of the fear attached to sharing my true emotions of the moment.

A recent *Forbes* article on understanding the white gaze defines it this way: "The white gaze can be expanded to mean the ways in which whiteness dominates how we think and operate within society. Being motivated to adhere to white-centered norms and standards is one of the ways that the white gaze operates."[3]

And this is what I am referring to. Is it okay to have time and space away from this gaze? How do we find it? What would it mean for the journey into self-love and joy? And piggybacking on the deep-listener lens in the last chapter, I now feel an even wider desire to peel myself away from this gaze, at least for longer than a few moments.

I have no real vested interest in changing or educating white folks about their inherent privileges. That's work they need to do on their own and from a place of sincerely wanting real change, for which they will have to commit to looking back, too. I have conversations with other creators of colour about this, often. But the emotional labour attached to diversity work triples when you are a writer. (I recall hearing Téa Mutonji say this in a CBC interview where she spoke about launching her short story collection.) And it's true. So when we think about the heavy weight of educating white folks on how they have to unlearn all the things, I have limits; I have to put myself first. My joy and ease of life as one unified goal holds so much more weight and power than trying to relieve white folks of their discomfort.

But I always welcome open dialogue as it connects to my own journey. I am and will always be the master of my experiences. I hold that knowledge close in times of strife, fear, and uncertainty. I recall speaking with a white male writer about my goal of wanting to live, love, and create with balance and in a healthy way. He said, "But don't you have that?" And it reminded me that the work we are doing to thrive won't be understood by everyone. Not everyone will see this work as a lifelong journey. But once again, language rises to the surface. **Moment to harvest: We have to expose the narratives that cause us to second guess our paths. Can we reimagine where we want to go?**

Meghan Watson says, "self-love to me is imagination. It's allowing ourselves to dream, hope, reimagine, reinvent, and redesign how we see ourselves." I too believe this thoroughly. And this inward work of establishing and acknowledging the sense of self doesn't end here. It follows me into the next chapter, where I explore a conversation that I've been having for forty years. Will I see you on the other side?

10

I Will Explore My POC Joy

"I grew up understanding myself as Black, I grew
up being named as Black. And to be read as Black
is a very particular experience, there is a very specific repertoire of hurt one feels when one is Black,
related to intelligence, related to beauty, related
to moral character, and I felt it acutely all of my
life growing up. It has shaped me fundamentally."
—David Chariandy, in conversation with the author, 2021

I feel better equipped to shed some other old beliefs and
unhealthy ways of thinking. This is what autumn is all
about. And why not solicit my moments of harvest from the
past two seasons? I've gained enough confidence to do this.
I've built a solid framework for a sense of self that is totally
preparing me for this work I'm about to do. I uncovered my
deep-listening skills too. Now, as I move into these complex
conversations, I know I have built some strength, maybe a bit
of resilience too.

"But you don't look *that* Black." During one of my very-first-ever public book readings, these were the first words uttered to me by the event organizer. Standing there in front of her, I felt myself shrink into my wobbly high-heeled shoes. Not only was it such an unexpected and offensive way to greet someone, but what in the world did it have to do with my participation in the event? Well, I could already predict how this was going to go. Let the derailment begin.

After the incredible "sense of self" conversations I've had with the Black leaders for this book, I want to take the opportunity to be more radical in this chapter and zero in on identity. I've spent my whole life cloaked in uncertainty around what it means to be Black. Excavating this has been a major hurdle on my path to joy. Whether it was me searching for my own face while watching TV with my family or building my circle of friends, I compared everything about myself to the world around me, and I worried that I wasn't good enough or that I didn't fit a specific mold. At times this made me feel incredibly sad, like there was something I was missing out on, something I couldn't name, that some secret was being kept from me, or that I didn't know how to just be.

I have one photo of my mom and dad that lives in a special folder inside my phone. It's the only picture I have of them *together*. I'm sure there are more in existence, but this is the only one I have. My mom is smiling and wearing a floral print dress, her small afro framing her face. She was a beauty at that moment. My dad, a South Asian East African man, is standing there with his hand on his hip, in tight white pants and a tropical shirt unbuttoned, his chest proudly exposed, his other arm wrapped around my mother's shoulders. I look at this photo often. I've attempted to take features from each of them and compare them to my own in a desperate scramble to figure out where I fit. As much as my path to joy is a lifelong journey, so is the unfolding and understanding of identity and all the various experiences that shaped *me*.

Halfway through the fall season, I felt compelled to escape to a hidden hiking trail steps from my home. After finding a flat spot to spread out a blanket, I opened my computer. Fall is the one season where I feel intuitive, and maybe that's connected to the planning I do in the fall. I couldn't name it, but at that moment, I knew something big was still yet to be uncovered.

I tucked the photo of Mom and Dad back into its virtual folder and got to work.

I can't shake the feeling of "not enoughness" that I feel inside my own Blackness. If I hadn't called on all the tools I've used so far, I could've derailed this journey to joy. I needed to start this pivotal conversation now, or everything could fall apart.

I found solace sharing this in conversation with prolific author David Chariandy. Identifying as Black is complex for us as two people with Black *and* South Asian ancestry. I've often been told that I cannot claim to be Black and mixed-race at the same time because I have to choose a way to identify. I asked him how he felt about this. It's not an easy question to ask or explore, and I feared there would never be an easy answer. I can predict that this is a conversation I'll be having for the rest of my life, and that tells me that I'll need to build up the strength to do it.

I had been looking forward to speaking with David Chariandy about self-love and joy for so long, but I was nervous about the work ahead of me. It's important to check in on ourselves in these moments. *Can I offer that to you, my readers, right now?*

I asked David about the first time he felt real joy, like deep down in his marrow, his earliest memories of it. And just like many of the others I spoke to, he paused. I have to acknowledge this. There's a pattern playing out here, in that joy is connected to space, time, and slowing down. When he told me about a memory of playing on a hill with his Trinidadian cousins, I relaxed, because my early memories were also starting to come back to me. I wanted to think about how we tether or untether ourselves to certain memories and why some are so crystal clear while others are fuzzy or blurry at best. I'm no expert here, but I think we bind ourselves to specific memories based on how we see ourselves inside of them. Oftentimes we aren't remembering it at all, but instead unconsciously revisiting the last time we *thought* about the memory. And when an experience is lost, talking about it is bringing back the memory of what was left behind. It's like what George Elliott Clarke says in his introduction to his book *Whylah Falls*: "[It] is the memory of what was omitted."[4] It's here that I often find myself.

David shared that he recalls only being two or three years old when his mother walked out of the hospital room carrying his new baby brother, and how he knew, in that moment, that his life was about to change. Imagine that realization at such a young age. Imagine feeling the world shift just slightly, maybe like a little earthquake—you feel it under your feet, you're sure you did, but you still question it. What was that? Did that just happen? Was it joy? Fear?

We are so inside of ourselves and our feelings at a young age because we don't yet experience the societal pressures around us to rush, to chase perfection, to change who we are. There aren't any old selves to shed yet. We are still hard at work seasoning our minds. Joy can be bred through change and growth.

What would it look like if, in our youth, we were all encouraged to seek out things that brought us joy versus being nudged in some random direction by those closest to us because they *think* that's what is best for us. Working toward self-love through an intimate exploration of identity has made me think about these possibilities.

I have to acknowledge that David's memories triggered my own. Ones I don't often think about. Memories I do not come into organically. When David shared his first memories of joy, I was immediately pulled back into my past. I thought about how, in my youth, my cousin, my brother, and I ripped down my mother's shower curtain so that we could use it as a makeshift sled to slide down an incredibly steep hill in our East Vancouver neighbourhood the day after a rare snowstorm. I do have fond memories from my youth connected to joy, but the very *first* memories of self-love were birthed *outside* of family interaction, and this has always bothered me and added to my sense of not belonging. But Meghan Watson shared something with me during our conversation that I needed to call on, a **moment to harvest: "Learning to love yourself is learning to let go of who you thought you should be. And you are building a sense of memory without** *tying anything* **to that memory."** This is a helpful piece of connective tissue for me because she is exactly right. My first memories of joy are not connected to familial rememberings, and that is okay. It's also okay to bring objectivity to that internal archive of self. This was a curious revelation.

At the end of spring, I spoke about the written word, and how finding a stack of old letters from my dad brought me much closer to joy. Why? Because my younger, twenty-something self was not ready to properly process the content of those letters—the answers to my questions around my father's history and lack of involvement in my life. The first time I read those letters, my insides were too tangled with anger and pain to properly assess the massive gifts my father was offering me on the page. More than a decade later, I read those same letters with the same eyes, but this time the words were filtered through a very different lens, a lens sculpted through years and years of mindset work, new experiences, self-trust, and growth. This, my friends—exploring the fractures and pain embedded around my identity—was the work of more than forty seasons.

Maybe I should talk about the complexities that can attach themselves to folks from two different marginalized groups—I have no idea why folks sometimes assume that "mixed-Black" means that the other "half" is white. When folks start the guessing game around who I am and who my parents are, the uncomfortable conversations begin.

David Chariandy knows that saying he is Black is housed within a profoundly intimate relationship with a particular South Asian experience, and as he puts it, "one of indenture, and a different type of migration experience than slavery, through colonialism, a legacy of struggle and suffering of its own."

In addition to speaking to the difficulties of coming from two different marginalized communities, David says there is a place, as Black people, to have real and honest conversations about hierarchies of privilege within the Black community, regarding the colour of skin—important discussions right alongside sexuality, gender, class: "I am all for that. But when someone says, 'But you are not quite Black or you are *half* black,' I want to push back and say no. That is not what shaped me."

Moment to harvest: That is not what shaped me. There it is. I put that gem in my pocket.

Like me, David also turns to other Black people, to other Black authors. He let go of how others saw him through his own engagement with Black people and Black art and Black

159

writing. "It's kind of weird hearing someone tell me that I am not quite the same as some other Black person. Notwithstanding, I want to recognize forms of privilege that I most certainly have." Although we didn't discuss what those privileges were, I think we, as mixed-race Black folks, have to be open to investigating and learning these privileges over time. Perhaps a seed for the next cycle. We all have such unique lived experiences that the timing won't be the same for all of us. This is part of the diversity of experiences I wanted to create space for.

I'm grateful for my guides, as they play a role in how far I've come. In thinking about the people, experiences, and books that shaped me, I recall all of the amazing authors whose writing I have found comfort in, especially those who speak to and explore the complex and layered experience of being "othered." Wayde Compton's *After Canaan: Essays on Race, Writing, and Region* is one of those books, a book that offered me new ways of thinking about the language we use to discuss race and ethnicity. Tessa McWatt's *Shame on Me: An Anatomy of Race and Belonging* is constructed using the unique container and close examination of the body. I turn to other Black writers, such as Ian Williams, Esi Edugyan, Robyn Maynard, and Toni Morrison, just to name a few. These writers' stories helped shape me too.

People have attempted to categorize and make assumptions about who I am and what spaces I belong in, and this has left painful traces of self-doubt that I carry with me. These traces are a part of me and contribute to my joy because I am not ignoring that pain nor am I attempting to set myself free from it completely. But what I've come to realize is that the unlearning of caring what people think is going to take at least a couple cycles. But I need to express gratitude toward David in this particular season. Autumn is the catalyst for this work of shedding old selves, and I know I've started to peel back the edges in a strategic way. This is work I can do alone and in the company of community. *Is this work you are ready to do too?*

And this is why community is so important, especially for Black folks. There will always be something different that shaped us, but we are still linked, whether through pain, problem, privilege, or joy. I don't have to fill a quota or meet a marker of Blackness. It's almost embarrassing to admit that I'd been carrying that fear around with me all these years. Time to let that go? Yes, I meant this as a question. My biggest gift on this journey so far is that I can let that fear go.

I felt lighter after speaking with David about the nooks and crannies of complex identity. Maybe it's because a big part of my joy is being able to feel more confident with my identity based on what's shaped me too. David and I both agreed that we are indeed part of a conversation that is expansive. We both ask ourselves of this so-called Black experience: How can we each contribute to that conversation based on our specific experiences and yet never come to assume that "I am *the* experience or I can represent *the* experience"? A question worthy of exploration over a lifetime. I do feel ready to continue this lifelong work. *Where are you and your expectations right now? What lifelong work will you have to continue carving a path for?*

But let's talk again about time. There is a sense of joy that comes just from having conversations and knowing that they don't have to be completely unpacked in a moment. It's work I can do, and at the end of the season, everything doesn't have to be solved. My joy is coming from knowing I can take my time with everything I do. I can slow down again and again. With writing, publishing, and running my own business, that realization that I don't have to rush opens so many doors, and folks better be on MY schedule. Going forward, fall may very well be the dedicated time for this identity exploration work. The soil feels just right for this kind of excavation. It's also perfect because I will also do my biggest shedding in the fall, and it's the most perfect prerequisite to collecting the wisdom I gain every cycle. As time moves forward, we mature, we learn, we let go. I can feel the intentional cadence of that. It's that sway that Maya Angelou spoke about. I think I finally have it.

When I signed up to take a mindfulness-based stress reduction course, I had no idea what to expect except that this was part of my journey to do things in a way that felt good for me. Initially I wanted to take it to further develop my professional skills so that I could add a layer of intentionality to the creative sustainability program I'd been building, but I ended up taking the lessons pretty personally. I showed up to each class with enthusiasm. Trust me. In this class there was a huge focus on slowing down, being in the moment, taking the time to acknowledge the people and world around us. I am so grateful for this. It was the catalyst for all the work I am doing, the work that will forever change the way I show up for myself.

I can see this other self much more clearly now. She's there. I'm here. I think the biggest fear I hold right now is that others who haven't seen the revolution unfold will challenge me. When they meet the changed me, they will say, "I don't know who you are." I have to prepare myself for that. But the responsibility is theirs. They have to relearn me and let go of that frozen image they have of me as the scared, quiet little girl, the image of me from when they held the most control over me. I speak to that girl often, but she's not the one taking this journey.

11

We Will Put Our Hands in Our Mothers' Gardens

As fall eases its way out, I feel hyper-aware of my environment. Vibrant colours shift to grey, and the reality of a cold winter grazes my neck. Before we move forward, we have an opportunity at the end of fall to look back.

Fifteen years ago, my son made me a round, concrete mosaic stone for Mother's Day. I recall carrying it home thinking, oh my gosh, why couldn't the teacher have prompted them to make something lighter? It was so heavy, and my forearms ached by the time I made it home and placed it in front of my door. I've never been one of those mothers who kept every single painting, drawing, or masterpiece their child made in class because I wanted the reflection, the looking back, to feel special, not overwhelming. In fact, I remember telling myself that I would keep one box of "memories," and once that box was full, that was it. The stone was special to me because it was such an unexpected creation. It wasn't a painting that could disintegrate in the Vancouver rain. It was sturdy, indestructible.

Because prioritizing is a major tool called upon this fall, I can see that it helped me early on, but it also helped me be more intentionally nostalgic. It's not as special when you have ... everything. Maybe this is an unpopular opinion, and that's okay.

I also knew I would never be a soccer mom. But I still felt the outside pressure to conform to that way of existing. You know, that smiling woman with all the *good* snacks, driving her kids to this activity and that, mapping out the family's schedule on some big white board in the kitchen. It wasn't in me and I just didn't connect with *that* image of motherhood. I often rolled my eyes at these women, and to be honest, I found their smiles suspect. I wondered if there was a hurt or a longing underneath those smiles. Again, my deep-listening superpower was in full effect. Drop me in a room for five minutes with a stranger, and I'll emerge with their heart's story without ever asking them a single question. There's a body language most people can't hide. I always see it. This is another weight to carry, though. Picking up on others' energies can be heavy, just like that mosaic stone.

I didn't want to be that mother who seemed to put herself last. And I was honestly afraid that I'd slip into this without realizing it. Instead, I dreamed of myself cooking in the kitchen with my child, setting up a camera and recording ourselves while we attempted to create some ridiculously complicated cupcake recipe—our own cooking show. I wanted both of us to benefit from being welcomed into each other's worlds. I imagined us flipping through books and trying to find ourselves within the pages. I predicted we would cry together when we spoke about the realities of the world today. I pictured us fastened in all the unspoken ways a child can bond with a mother. I chose to show my son the power of chasing dreams and loving the self the whole way through, even when love didn't seem like an option for me or when I didn't know how to describe it. This didn't always work out as planned. There was just way too much self-doubt on my shoulders as a new mom trying to find her way in the world and within the self.

So how could I model self-love for him when I was still figuring it out for myself? Was it okay to include him on this journey?

If there's one thing I'm sure about, it's that young people are vigilant. They are paying close attention to how we look in the mirror and the words we use with ourselves. I'm glad I started to change my language in the past couple of seasons. Suddenly, those soccer mom qualities felt less concerning. I wanted my son to see me in the fullest of joy, my authentic self. I also wanted him to see what made me sad and that it's natural to feel disconnected from joy too. I wanted him to see that we are the only ones in control of our own happiness. I wanted him to see me step back from spaces and people that made me uncomfortable. I wanted him to see me creating safer spaces for myself and leaning into my deep-listening superpowers, which is something he, at twenty years old, now holds too. But sometimes I gave in and showed up at the sporting events, my collar pulled up around my neck as the wind pushed itself in through my thin jacket. I went to the pep rallies, and BBQs.

Nothing was lost from attending these kinds of events, but not much was gained either. My son thought I wanted him to be there taking part in these events, and I thought he wanted me there, observing. In reality, we both would have rather been at home doing our own thing. Finding this out over a random conversation one night was almost a sigh of relief. Hilarious that we were both showing up for each other in the wrong ways. We can laugh about that now. #JoyInTheMistakes. But this is why our seasonal tools are so powerful. *How have you been using your tools?*

When I had my child at twenty-one years old, I had no idea what kind of mother I wanted to be. But I did know that I wanted to make decisions based on what made sense for *me* and not allow unwanted advice to permeate my being. I did know that my child would have their own likes and dislikes early and that it was up to me to acknowledge these and treat my child as an individual, as a human being. For me, motherhood started when I realized that my life would be forever changed, just like David Chariandy shared about having a new sibling. I was open to all the possibilities that this change might bring. But motherhood is not the only thing I want to talk about here. I want to put three cards on the table, line them up, and examine them.

Card one: When I was young, I often had to take care of myself and worry about my mother. This wasn't fun at seven years old or at thirteen or at seventeen. But I can see now that

I was unknowingly preparing myself for something much bigger.

Card two: After I moved out and was living on my own, I had my child three years later. I loved every moment with this tiny human and vowed to show up in the best way I could. I went from one caretaking role directly into another. Looking back now, I can hardly believe this was twenty years ago.

Card three: Here, I predict the future. Having a partner eighteen years older than me makes me aware of my next caretaking role to come. I've spent forty years in a caretaking role, but I haven't been putting myself first as much as I should have. I think many of us have felt this in our daily lives. But this is work I have been committed to over the last few years. This was a heavy realization and one I am grateful for, because what better time to begin to focus on myself and to prepare for everything ahead? It's true, I didn't "take time to find myself" or backpack in Europe (do people really do that?!), or any of those coming-of-age happenings that I only saw in movies. I spent my life making sure everyone else was okay. Being in a caretaking role is unpredictable, uncertain. But it is the most powerful life role I've held, and I know I am stronger for it.

During my 2018 book launch, my then sixteen-year-old relayed to the world that he identified as trans. Although I was proud of him for sharing this and for doing so with extreme pride, I was worried about not knowing how to be a mother, again. What would motherhood look like now? Looking back now, I can see the seasons were my guide. There is always an opportunity to start fresh, reassess the foundation, and dig my fingers in that soil again. I could build my own garden for this mothering. I could, at the very least, plan for what I wanted it to look and feel like. I had to hold that knowledge close to my heart. This new chapter for him wasn't about me, I knew that then and I know it now. But there was still a fear of getting it wrong, again. But it's language that can further guide us, because calling in open and honest conversation is where we should try to start from. It wasn't my job to educate my wider family or predict how they would react. My son had me as a pillar, and if no one else wanted to do the work to understand and educate themselves, then that was their burden to carry. I was here to support my son whichever way he needed. All he had to do is ask. But as deep listeners, asking can be difficult to achieve. **Moment to harvest: Asking is not always as easy as just pushing the words out.** More work to do here. I put this in my pocket.

As we climb out of fall and lean into winter, the amount of time I spend inside my head will increase, and believe it or not, I look forward to this now. I can tuck myself away and look at all the wisdom I've harvested. I can compare what's different and more robust than previous cycles. And now, that willingness to let go of old parts of the self does feel a bit easier. I am grateful for the conversations I've had, especially with Meghan Watson. Sometimes it can feel like my epiphanies or aha moments come out of nowhere, but really, it's due to me being a slow processor. We need time to absorb knowledge and for our bodies to hold it. And if one of my initial goals was to slow down, well hey, I'm right on track, then.

I think back to asking that room full of writers what their definition of failure was. Everyone had their own laundry list of what failure entailed. I am always amazed at how writers can be so creative, even when it comes to talking about something as terrifying and all-encompassing as failure. Now, in holding all of the ideas, learnings, experiences, and tools I've gathered lovingly thus far, I ask myself that same question and wonder if it is possible to feel and experience the joys of motherhood alongside the fear of failure and getting it wrong.

What does it look like to be a mother of a trans son who is now slowly but inevitably venturing into adulthood? What did I have to unlearn about myself and about what being a mother looked like? What belief systems did I have to let go of, and what milestones would I no longer have access to? Could I be a mother when I felt I didn't experience a specific version of motherly guidance as a child? Could I build my own traditions if none were passed down to me? After asking these bold questions, fall showed itself in all its colourful glory. I've spent years mothering, and through this experience, I've matured enough to see new paths unfold before me. There were so many possibilities presenting themselves to me, and fall was the perfect time to listen.

When my son turned nineteen, I began to worry about how slowly he was moving out of that adolescence phase. I wanted to support him without crossing boundaries. I read as widely as I could and stumbled upon *Failure to Launch* by Mark McConville, who notes that "more twentysomethings than ever before are struggling with the transition to adulthood as a result of more parental engagement (aka helicopter parenting), a more challenging economic environment... and big changes in cultural norms... Kids today worry more and risk less—there are huge increases in anxiety and depression among young people today."[5] And when I considered this, alongside the added complexity he had navigating life as a tri-racial trans young person, I knew my son had more on his plate than either of his parents had ever considered. There is always going to be work to do, and I am here for it. Maybe my role wasn't to try to find a solution for him, but instead to show him that the work of self-love is constant, and it's often the place we have to start. I do believe that wisdom can develop its purest form from hardship. The more I listened to fall—leaves shuttling to the ground, raspy winds—and felt warm wool curled around my body, the more I could see that the shape of me as mother is just as unique as my joy-discovery. *How can the caregivers build their own paths to joy?*

Before working on this path to joy and, essentially, a sense of self, I would carry with me extreme pangs of guilt for not adhering to that soccer mom image of motherhood, even though in the early years, I forced myself into that narrative. We want to do what we think is best for our children, but do we ever, without doubt, respect that they are individuals too?

I remember rereading *The Autobiography of My Mother*, an incredibly poetic and lush novel by Jamaica Kincaid, and being completely engrossed in her depiction of her character's vision of being a mother and the difference between being a mother and bearing children. That's not to say I shared that same outlook, but what interested me was the fact that this viewpoint was so different from what we see and hear in pop culture and, heck, even from what we share in conversation with our closest circles. In her novel, Kincaid's character says:

> I would never become a mother, but that would not be the same as never bearing children. I would bear children, but I would never be a mother to them. I would bear them in abundance; they would emerge from my head, from my armpits, from between my legs; I would bear children, they would hang from me like fruit from a vine, but I would destroy them with the carelessness of a god. I would bear children in the morning, I would bathe them at noon in a water that came from myself, and I would eat them at night, swallowing them whole, all at once.[6]

There is such beauty in the honesty of these words. So confident. It's the confidence in knowing who she is and what she is capable of that I am drawn to. What does it mean for me to be a mother? Who gets to decide?

When Shakura and I were speaking on the phone to get to know each other before our event, she asked me how long I'd been a Black woman. I was frozen for a second. What answer did she want? Why did she ask this? What if I got it wrong? This late in the season and I was still filled with fear. I told her I didn't have an answer, that what has shaped me (thank you, David, for that harvest) was connected to who I was, and to who I wasn't. When I consider my own mother, I am often curious about what goes on in her head. What is she thinking about in the moments when she's quiet? What is she thinking about when she's alone? What are her greatest hopes? Can she even see that far or has she never thought to look? Does she hold a definition of joy for herself? Does she know what makes her feel alive, even if that feeling is temporary? I can't say I've ever asked her. I'm not ready for the answers.

For the mothers: Can we create a new way of mothering that connects to joy, feels unique to us as individuals, and showcases all the different sides, bumps, curves of self that we've come to know and love? Is it okay to love differently? I told y'all I write to unearth questions! And not all questions can be answered in one book.

How do we as parents instill a sense of joy in being Black? I feel lucky to have been in conversation with Alexandra Elle, author of *After the Rain* and *How We Heal*. When I think about honest self-love and not being afraid to step back and say "No, this is not what I need," I think of Alex. She tells me that joy and a sense of pride in being Black was not something she grew up with. In fact, she thought that being Black was a negative thing. "Nobody was celebrating Blackness when I was coming up in my family," she said. Of course, this makes me think about how we mother our children when these belief systems are in place. I wonder, is it possible to unlearn and relearn?

Alex came into her own traditions and beliefs when she met her husband, who *did* grow up celebrating his Blackness. "Being married to someone who was raised in a pro-Black household has done us so well. Our children look so different, we are a melting pot, but we are Black and we are celebrating Blackness in this house, and our children will know you are Black and you are proud."

Before writing this chapter, I felt like I had failed as a mother because that soccer mom image continued to haunt me. But Alex is the perfect example of how unlearning and choosing to build something new is the way we bust open old stereotypes and find our own cracks of joy. "We have our own traditions, we are teaching them their history, and it is such a beautiful thing to give our children what I didn't have. They will never not love themselves. They see their daddy loving their Black mama, they hear us talking about how beautiful Black people are. My identity has shifted, thinking it was the bottom of the barrel to be Black, and to be where I am now, I would never want my children to feel how I felt. It starts at home."

Moment to harvest: Joy starts at home. It starts with the self.
Adding this to my pocket.

So why is it so difficult for me to picture Black mothers and joy? Is it because the world does not believe that Black women should or could be happy? Is it because the media wants to keep alive the stereotypes of the Black woman forever burdened? Is it because motherhood is something we endure versus experiencing it with happiness and curiosity? But remember, that of all the unlearnings and letting go, I knew the belief that the hard experiences were connected to me being a Black woman was going to be the biggest unravelling of them all. Here we are at the end of fall and I'm no closer to the answer. But I will keep digging.

For a *Washington Post* article, Krissah Thompson asked Black mothers how they find their joy. The responses fill my cup. Leslie O'Neill said, "We don't see joy reflected in popular culture, so we make our own." Keila Dumas said, "I find joy in knowing that I get a chance to create my own narrative not only for myself as a mother, but for my child. I embrace my intersectionality."[7] It's fulfilling to know that we are having this conversation and that we can write our own narratives, because the joy I've found in being a mother is that I can influence a young person's life and *guide* them. I don't have to watch them kick a soccer ball to know I'm a mama. I can bear children. And I can be a mother. *Dear reader, I feel the need to check in on you. How can the fall help you to pay attention to the parts of you that you've spent a lifetime getting to know? Who can you be?*

I feel like a changed person having had the opportunity to spend an hour speaking about Black self-love and joy with Anais Granofsky, who as a youngin' starred in the original *Degrassi Junior High* TV series. Listen, even her voice made me feel that the person in front of me was someone who I should be sure to pay close attention to. I wasn't expecting to start my conversation with Anais on the topic of motherhood, but believe it or not, it became the entire thread. This felt natural, so I threw my questions out, and leaned in. We spoke about how teaching our children about gratitude could open them up to seeing the world in a different way. Not everyone gets that space to be creative, to slow down. Her mom had creativity and wanted to be a writer and wasn't able to.

I think we can carry a trapped pain on behalf of our mothers. Maybe it's knowing what they always wanted to do but didn't. Or couldn't. We might carry this because of the guilt we feel for doing all the things they didn't do. But this leads us to look further into memory and to look at the images that we carry forever. The way we carry memory has always fascinated me because it can shapeshift over time. The images we carry in our minds trigger memories, and this becomes a great way to slow down. We can zoom into these images and ask questions of them. What feelings or emotions are present inside these images? In the short documentary film *In Our Mothers' Gardens* directed by Shantrelle Lewis, there is a complex exploration of the vastly different relationships between Black mothers and Black daughters. There is no template, and I felt a deep sense of relief in knowing this. In the film, one woman spoke about still learning her mother after thirty-seven years. Learning a mother over a lifetime means you have no choice but to slow down. And that has been the focus of much of this book. For the most part, our mothers were trying to survive. This reality validated my desire to want more than that. This notion of thriving was speaking loudly, and as I've been doing throughout this journey, I had to slow down to hear all the nuances of this particular song that we call motherhood. As one woman said in the documentary, "You can't have a short memory and be Black. You open yourself up for attack. You gotta have a long memory because you're singing a long song."[8] I think it's important that we interpret that for ourselves.

When writing her own book, *The Girl in the Middle*, Anais Granofsky had the opportunity to interview her parents, and not as the naïve, wounded child, but as a writer. She could interview them as people. For the first time.

What she learned is that they were just trying their best, just like we are trying our best. There's definitely joy in acknowledging that fact, in respecting that effort, no matter the outcome. Fall reminds us of this. Things are dying, but there's a rebirth coming.

Anais shared with me an intimate moment with her mom during a telephone conversation where they said every mean thing they'd been intentionally holding on to. I had to pause and picture this for myself. What was I holding on to that maybe my own mother needed to hear? In my moment of pause, I was able to look back at the work I've already done around reimagining a relationship with my own mother. I started to see that I had to let go of the expectations I had for my mother. The things I wanted her to do and say were all things she was not capable of. I don't mean this in a negative way, but I honestly have to wait for her to take her own journey, just as I am taking mine. Anais told me that she and her mother exhausted themselves and the pain came out like a monsoon. At the end of the call, she told her mother she loved her and they hung up. The relationship shapeshifted into a splendid thing from that moment on. That anger was in the way, and when they finally said it, they got past something. It was unexpected and opulent.

I didn't mean to summarize Anais's experience, but it wasn't mine to stretch out. But I can relate to this full circle moment. Anais and her mother couldn't have gotten there without the ugly releasing. It was like purging. A letting go. Joy can be on the other side. Maybe it's as simple as saying let's get this out of the way. Can joy be that quick? That simple?

Through Anais, I can imagine a future where I can ask my own mother what she needs to be happy. I learned that I may never be ready to do this particular bit of work—at least not this season. I also remind myself that it's okay. I have to acknowledge all of the work I've done so far. And I have to remember that it is lifelong. I can have a strained relationship with her and still love her fiercely. Joy is coming. Joy has always been here. Joy is inside of me.

Fall *Un*learnings

LET'S UNLEARN:
SELF-LOVE SHOULD BE IMMEDIATE AND LINEAR.

Self-love can take its time; it's not always urgent. It's also not always going to be clear what self-love looks like for us, especially if we've never directly addressed this for ourselves. I tell y'all, I am so happy to unravel this convoluted self-work and I feel so much stronger for it. What I've also made space for by unlearning the whole "self-love is immediate" nonsense is that each season, I can reassess the ways in which I love myself. What can I prioritize each and every season? So much power in this revelation.

LET'S UNLEARN:
FITTING A MOLD = BELONGING.

We have to look at what it feels like to belong within ourselves first. Without that foundational work done, how dare we tell someone they don't belong? I'm not here to make assumptions about people anymore; it's not healthy. We also can't assume that you can shove a group of people who look alike in a room, close the door, and expect an immediate bond or connection. Belonging happens through a desire to feel safe, heard, and respected on our own terms. That is often something that, like self-love, happens over time.

LET'S UNLEARN: THERE ARE EASY ANSWERS TO IDENTITY CONVERSATIONS.

This is the biggest unlearning of the season for me, and I cannot even begin to tell you how much lighter I feel. I will forever be inside this conversation. It is complex work. The slowing down I've allowed myself will definitely play a role in this unlearning. I have to make the time and space to do this work, and that means consistent letting go and release will become a part of my routine. It's okay for this exploration to be lifelong work, and that is the biggest relief. We don't have to have all the answers.

LET'S UNLEARN: EVERYTHING CAN BE SOLVED IN A SINGLE SEASON.

Oh, friends! This is life work. I know I am committed to consistently repeating and relearning, but I hope to figure out how

I can call others into this revelation. As Black women especially, we put a lot of pressure on ourselves to be strong, to fix everything in our families, to be the hero. This is what I know I have to unlearn but it's going to take community, and heck, it might take some time to huddle. So I say, let's take it one season at a time.

LET'S UNLEARN: SURVIVAL MODE IS THE SAME AS THRIVING.

Huge one, friends. We are not thriving when we can barely get out of bed because we worked ourselves too hard the day before. I spent my entire life "just getting by," putting my dreams on hold to help someone else, or denying myself the things I wanted because I didn't think I deserved them. Those days are fading away. I am ready to thrive. I am ready to finally start my journey of living. Y'all here for it?

Was there anything you weren't ready to let go of? Carry it forward into the winter.

Don't forget to revisit the cyclical questions from the community call to carry you forward:

- What do I need or want to make space for right now?

- How am I really feeling? I want to be honest about my feelings with myself and others.
- What feels heavy? I want to try to let go of this by season's end.

"**Cultivating joy is not a linear process. We must protect our joy and meet ourselves with gratitude, patience, and love.**"

—Paris Alexandra

Winter Community Call:

Building a Dream Home

Our final community call, y'all, and winter is here. My tools for this season's work will include taking everything I've learned and unlearned . . . and building a home. In this home (a physical home and a home with self), can I start to rediscover joy? There's something about winter and preparation for the final unlearning . . .

REMINDER

Where are we now? How did we get here? Let's celebrate the big decisions we've made, despite the hurdles of youth, family, and identity we explored in the previous seasons. How can we explore our own definition of welcoming spaces to help us build a home within ourselves?

Can we really let go?

LET'S FOCUS

At the beginning of each season, I call on all of you to ask yourselves the same three questions:

- What do I need or want to make space for right now?
- How am I really feeling? I want to be honest about my feelings with myself and others.
- What feels heavy? I want to try to let go of this by season's end.

12

Down Payment: Get Your Entrepreneurial Mind Right

Winter is about dreaming and getting lost in the inner workings of our own minds. Winter is for planning and bolstering projects (for me, that means my business). Winter is about paying close attention to what our bodies are telling us as they react to the changing climate. But we have to remember to pull out our tools too. It was only recently that I started to look at what it meant to find home. I fell into the realization that home is not only a physical space but a combination of spaces, feelings, people, and beliefs that allow me to feel safe and secure. While I journey into what it means to be home, I call on the chill of winter to grant me the necessary time and space tucked away to sculpt my business and make some really big decisions that will either make or break my entrepreneurial spirit. *Consider something big and buried in your life that you want to uncover. You don't have to*

be a business owner to find the space for dreaming this winter.
Where is your heart right now?

One of my fondest memories of being young is how I adored organizing. It was joy-inducing for sure, and still is. I always sought out the most efficient way to do something. Whether it was sorting my books by genre or organizing drawers and closets, I found it calming to have control over my space, to always know where everything was, and to be able to plan what was going to happen next. I had control over the position of my belongings. I could count on knowing where they were and therefore be able to weather uncertainty as it showed up.

But where did this come from? Growing up, I was not surrounded by entrepreneurial role models, but I did love this idea of happiness being connected to control around the choices I made; complete autonomy was a goal for me from birth. I know it was; it still is. I want to wake up when I want to wake up. Maybe it was in the air or simply an intuition, but I knew as a young woman that if I was going to be happy, I needed to have a say in the work I did, and better yet, build it myself.

I'd already read quite a few good business books when I came across this standout: Rachel Rodgers's *We Should All Be Millionaires: A Woman's Guide to Earning More, Building Wealth, and Gaining Economic Power*. Even though I didn't connect to the language of "millionaires," I still wanted to check her out. Her membership club of the same name was where my dreams really took off. After joining her club for a year, working through her courses and stellar resources, and being a part of a like-minded community of women who were motivated and passionate AF, my core purpose really became clear.

In the fall of 2021, I was one of six women invited to attend a two-night retreat at Rachel Rodgers's ranch in North Carolina. The retreat offered an opportunity to step back from all the pressures and responsibilities back home. Because of Covid, with me living in Canada and international travel being difficult, I couldn't attend. Imagine my pain in having to say no to this opportunity! But that didn't mean I wasn't going to pay close attention to what I did have access to. 'Cause that's what entrepreneurs do, right? We pivot.

In her book, Rachel not only creates a tangible map to success, but she systemically breaks down why the Black woman has always been steps behind and how to begin to work toward climbing ahead and closing that racial wealth gap. I adored how she allowed us into her own personal experiences too. Rachel wasn't born into wealth; she worked hard. She was strategic. She took risks. She speaks about her own struggles and how building things her way just worked. I felt at home inside this book. Even though being a millionaire is not something I have ever considered to be the solution to my problems, nor is it something that I think will bring me happiness, I do know that feeling financially secure is a huge goal for me and for my family. Although I'm quite confident that I could have found security in the stability of a nine-to-five job, I knew I'd be ignoring a part of myself that wanted to build something much bigger than myself. I would have been ignoring the voice and the desire to build systems and processes that started from a place of intersectional care, love. The "not enough" of the nine-to-five was not something I could have continued to just power through. And yeah, I was part of the discussions with friends with nine-to-fives who also had dreams of doing their own thing: "But I'm not ready yet," or "I prefer the stability of my day job," or "Maybe I'll just stay in the side hustle mode." (I hate the term *side hustle*, by the way. Even the language makes me feel exhausted and burnt out!). I know how easy it is to forever stay spinning inside the dream mode. Dreaming is integral to the entrepreneurial Black female, but knowing when to exit that phase and turn dreaming into action is the part not many of us know how to do. How can you take a dream and push it into manifestation and implementation? We don't do enough dreaming as creatives, and we definitely don't do it enough as business owners.

Rachel Rodgers is someone I admire because of how she talks about potential paths for those who have been historically disadvantaged; she speaks often about how constructing a business is far more realistic to generate sustainable wealth than saving or climbing a corporate ladder. So this path to building a sustainable business started to feel intentional. Maybe I was onto something. But the journey is always riddled with barriers. And before I can power ahead, I have to look back. Before

I launched my own business, I was so tired of being tired. I no longer had the energy to take on roles within organizations that didn't yet have the resources I needed in order to thrive.

Burnout is not a new topic for me. In fact, I built my literary studio Breathing Space Creative as a response, and possible solution, to the burnout my peers and I were feeling on the daily. I recall people furrowing their brows when I started talking about author care and wellness for writers. But I persevered. And I have to say, I find it interesting that it took a global pandemic for people to recognize that, hey, maybe Chelene was onto something and writers do need added care and support. Yes, folks were tired, their lives were turned upside down, and the way we all communicated was turned on its head. And sure, writers and creators were not the only ones affected by the woes of Covid, but it did help people see how my vision to pre-emptively care for the storytellers—whom we still expected to show up and show out and expend their energy toward the glare of the Zoom screen instead of a live audience—was integral. We couldn't continue to expect storytellers to push through their traumas, their insecurities, their uncertainties without added support.

I started out as a consulting biz, helping small publishers provide added support to their authors through event prep, time-management help, and more. But it was much more time consuming than I had anticipated trying to convince publishers that this was a necessary service, that the storyteller was more important than the story. Folks weren't ready yet. I even recall one publisher telling me there would be "too many cooks in the kitchen." So after being tired of the rigidity, I rebranded and shifted my focus to work with individual writers. I figured, the writer knows best what the writer needs, and so starting to work with folks *before* they published became my focus. Through blog posts, a new podcast, one-on-one coaching, nourishment calls, and The Forever Writers Club, I was well on my way to helping authors build up a healthy mind and body to be able to not only take on the ups and downs of the publishing world, but also find balance and joy. 'Cause, y'all, none of us should be denied that. Enter The Thrive coaching program for creatives. Joy became a major goal for me and the writers I worked with. And what I quickly realized was that not all writers had publishing as an end goal. These writers deserved care too. Maybe there are writers out there who want writing and creation as an everyday part of their lives. How could I help them build a practice or a path to becoming a forever writer? I have Rachel Rodgers to thank for her Glow Up course, which allowed me the tools and knowledge to build up my business framework for The Forever Writers Club.

This was the framework I used when building free resources, paid services, and promo materials. Going forward, every program I built had its own unique framework. I lived this. I practised what I preached. And when balance started to show up in my own creative life, I was thrilled. But y'all, as we know, there's always someone out there ready to clap back our joy, or worse yet, question it. When my own balance and joy shows up unexpectedly, I do fear people saying, "How dare she have balance when I don't have it?" But I can let that go too. I have worked way too hard to let people take anything else from me. This is my heart work.

My joy and balance are now non-negotiable, a tool we picked up in the fall. I will never apologize for feeling good or for feeling and reveling in the moments when I have it all together. This isn't a constant, so you better believe that when I am cradled in the crevices of joy, Imma stay there for as long as I can stand it.

I built my own business because I wanted to find a space in publishing where I belonged, a space where I could thrive and grow and use *all* my expertise and experience. I wanted a place where I could not only use my skill set but do the work that was important to me and that brought me . . . joy. When Shakura S'Aida told me that she wanted to keep me safe, I knew I was valued. But thinking about her now, close to the end of our first cycle of seasons, I recognize that all of my guides are a bit quieter now. Maybe they see my growth and they know they can step back. Maybe they can see that my self-trust is growing.

But it wasn't easy to build something for myself. Self-doubt and negative self-talk permeated my body. Who am I to do this work? Fear, anxiety, and even bouts of depression are all things small business owners may butt heads with along the way. For me as a Black woman, proving myself was the biggest point of anxiety. In her viral *Globe and Mail* article "Black on Bay Street," Hadiya Roderique says, "I was a lawyer and I belonged there. But it felt like I had to prove it more, while others got the benefit of the doubt."[1]

So where is the joy, then? Why put ourselves in front of people and situations that make us feel less than or not enough? Although each of my conversations with the Black leaders were unique in their own way, I feel like everyone shared the same underlying value: that we are worthy of feeling happiness in a way that works for us, no matter what our past has done to us or what our present offers us. So I'm holding that learning. And friends, I'm raising the stakes. I am committing to surrounding myself with people who get me and my goals and *genuinely* want to be a part of my success and me theirs. There will always be people who—even if they do not realize it—want to find ways to amplify *why* you do not deserve that joy. When I share the good things that happen in my business, I want someone who leans in with curiosity instead of disbelief. Even this finding of community has been an uphill battle, I have to acknowledge the work I've done around mindfulness and self-care. My mind and body are my vessels for this work. I can't forget that. *Maybe you can look at your current boundaries or work relationships and map out what you really have control over. What can you change or let go of?*

What I've learned from the Black leaders so far is how great it is to say no to things and appreciate the things we say yes to. Every day I wake up and do this work, I give myself a small piece of the childhood that I never really had. There's power and a heck of a lot of joy in that.

I started to see a pattern of giving back to my younger self and catching sight of it spreading out into the community. This pattern is so graceful in all its brilliant, bright colours.

13

Pour the Foundation:
Black Male Joy

Arriving here, at this point in the book, I looked back at my own footprints pressed into the soil—soil that was covered in fresh white snow. When I bent down and looked closely at those prints, they were so well-defined, firm. With my footprints clearly lined behind me, I could see how far I'd walked and how close I was to feeling safe enough to say that I understand what is possible for me and my own joy, and for those who are closest to me. I am responsible for my own happiness; yes, this is true. But the arteries of my joy are bound to the people I hold close, just like those branches I spoke about before. But now those branches are bare and exposed to the weather. It's easy to feel sad about this exposure to the environment and its elements. I've learned and unlearned so much this cycle. But through all the open and honest conversations I've had, I could also sense a slight hesitation inside of myself, a holding back even though I was unsure of where this hesitation was coming from.

Who will you turn to as you investigate your own joy? Who are your guides? For me, I feel as though Ian Williams will speak the loudest here, and I have to remind myself that I can use my new deep-listening superpower to pay attention to what his words are doing for me. His book *Disorientation* was the first book written by a Black male about existing as a Black male that I could not put down. How was it that I could see myself in his narrative? I can't say I have the answer for that just yet, but that's part of the work I'm here to do. My tool this season is to take my unlearnings to date and build that sense of home. So let's go ahead and do that.

I had a feeling early on that writing about my hopes for the Black men in my life was going to be a difficult chapter for me because it's an opportunity to step back from my own narrative (a comfort zone of sorts!) and be vulnerable in a space that has often brought me discomfort, for reasons I've not explored. So I'm sure you can see why I am calling my guide in close. But hey, I'm not going to just toss out all the tools I've given myself. I'm not going to just suddenly forget everything I've learned up until this point. Resting and self-care defined by me will always be a top priority. So let me go ahead and flip that fear narrative for a minute and bring in the revision of language.

Writing this chapter is an opportunity to rest, to look at other stories outside of my own but still be tethered to them. (Note to self: good call saving this chapter for winter because I knew I'd be tucked away somewhere in reflection mode.) Winter always makes me think about uncomfortable things, and that's a part of what the weather wants us to know. We feel the elements trying hard to penetrate our skin. I don't want to get too personal here, because I promised y'all we wouldn't stay in those moments long. Can I use the tools I've shared with all of you to not only uplift Black men but also reimagine the future of my own relationships with them? I can't help but feel blessed by the Black men in my own family who've taught me so much about love.

I need the guidance of winter for this specific task of reimagining. The way the slow sun melts the snow is a reminder of the temporariness of this season. I should be spending time celebrating all the decisions I've made to date. I should be looking back at the pile of wisdom I've collected. And shouldn't I feel lighter, not only from all the old selves I've shed but from the unlearnings? Oh, the unlearnings. The cool air should be a bold reminder to stay alert, stay focused. So here, in this chapter, I dream. But I don't dream for myself. This is what the cool, crisp air reminds me of right now, that I can retreat into myself and dream, but I can dream for my community too.

Up until now, for the most part, I've been focusing on women: our stories, our voices, our bonds. The old spring version of me wants to apologize for that, but when I slowed down and evaluated my footprints, I realized that speaking to all the women is just what I needed to do this cycle. This doesn't mean that these tools cannot be picked up and used by men, just as Ian's book about being a Black male has reached me, a Black woman, in unexplainable ways. It was a tool I chose to pick up. Perhaps next year, next cycle, will call me to do very different work. These are the unknowns, the possibilities that excite me.

Winter is fragile. I never want to force anything. Icicles can break with the slightest push, but here I saved intentional space to reimagine and strengthen my relationships with Black men. I'll admit, it's a small space here in this chapter, but I have to start somewhere.

One thing I've learned amongst all the unlearning is that I must think about my own individual contribution as a unique key, and everyone has their own unique key. When we show up in certain spaces, what we contribute depends on our key. Yes, the collective work of coming together as a community is always going to play an integral role in any larger collaborative goal, but this *dreaming*, it's going to start with the self. It has to. But there's another important step I want to implement now: an assessment of my own energy. How much do I really have to give right now? Am I capable of cutting open old memories of pain, violence, and even death? No. Not this cycle. I cannot apologize for this. I won't. And yet, it's another sign that this work is ever-evolving. But does not talking about these things, specifically about the uncle who was taken from me and my family through police violence, mean I am ignoring a particular pain? Or am I assessing my own limits and respecting them in context of this book and where I am now? Is this the space to force out a story that maybe doesn't fit here right now? *I call y'all to breathe that in for yourselves right now.*

When I think about many of the Black men I've met in my life, I have to wonder: Is there some medium through which the pressures of being young, Black, and male have been explored? Is there a space or a vessel where young Black men have compiled, sculpted, and released their stories, individual struggles, barriers, and feelings? I know that there have been attempts through various films, books, and event podcasts. But I didn't know how to connect to any of this. Maybe this is why I've connected so intimately to Ian's book. To me, putting himself on the page in the way he did translated as a certain, very specific strand of joy. It was like music. I think back to the influence music had over me as a young girl and how positive it was for me. I recall turning up my favourite songs when I didn't have the words to communicate what was happening in my head. I can picture myself falling inside the warm crevices of a drum beat or bassline. Is there some way through which Black men have expressed honest fears?

When it comes to some Black males trying to sort out how to step out of their circumstances, I think about music: the trap genre in general was used by some Black communities as an outlet. In her article for Berklee Online, Ashley Pointer helps clarify why the unique music form is *called* trap. "A trap by standard definition is a device or enclosure designed to catch and retain typically by allowing entry but not exit."[2] *Catch, retain, allow entry, but not exit.* This reminds me of fishing. A fish biting a hook out of hunger and having it forever clutching the inside of the mouth, holding it there. Fighting one's way off the hook would cause so much physical damage, a looming danger, it makes more sense to stay stuck than try to escape. And I've seen other ways Black men have tried to get unstuck. I've been in conversations with Black men about the stigma connected to going to therapy, and although they could see the benefits of untangling and letting go of the hurts they've carried for so long, they didn't always see a safe space to start.

The indirect conversation around me as it relates to Black men hasn't always been positive. I don't enjoy the way these stereotypes fester: Black men as absent, as disengaged fathers, as immersed in crime, as self-absorbed, as hyper-masculine, as violent. Some of the women I know have been upset about how they were been treated or how their expectations were not met or how the Black men in their lives were "all the same." There's a specific hurt here and a penetrating sadness. How can this be the story of every Black man? It can't be. And I know that it isn't, but how did we get here? How can I use my tools to help unlearn this? And then what happens when we turn on the TV, and that narrative is splayed open, highlighted, and reinforced? Why is this the only story? It's like Chimamanda Ngozi Adichie said in her TED Talk "The Danger of a Single Story," "Show a people as one thing, only one thing, over and over again, and that is what they become."[3] I think there's a reason why videos like hers now have over 34 million views on YouTube. We know there is work to be done to change this narrative, and so we watch that video over and over in hopes that we will find the answer there. Lurking. Waiting.

Where do we start?

My tool this season is to utilize my *un*learnings and build a home. But let me also seek out the altering of language too. What if we begin to reframe the language we use with and about Black men, early on? What if we reimagine the roles for Black men in movies and as characters in the books we write?

In a *Teen Vogue* article on the movie *Moonlight* and a new era for queer Black men, Prince Shakur wrote, "As a queer black man, I've found solace in recent years from seeing many of my own experiences fearlessly reflected by those like [actor] Lonsdale and [rapper] Abstract. This is not only because such representation helps queer black men feel affirmed and powerful in their queerness, but because it also creates a reality where we are allowed to live outside the confines of black hypermasculinity and the whitewashing of the queer experience."[4] Representation matters. This we know. And what Shakur says about creating a reality for queer Black men to live outside of the confines of hypermasculinity hits differently in my chest. I think that's exactly it. What if the Black men we see in pop culture could indeed be devoid of all the stereotypes that have followed them for much too long? We have control over how, what, and who we shape and highlight. We have control over the language we use. What if we dreamed a new language for them? I know my contribution. This work absolutely has to start with the self. We focus on what we have control over.

———

In his *Washington Post* article on Black men and masculinity, Andre M. Perry says, "Our culture of hypermasculinity hits black men hard, prizing dominance, sexual prowess and aggression—qualities that impede honest communication and healthy intimate relationships."[5] But how do we let Black men *know* that we are here for a different narrative? Maybe it's in how we respond to their gentle acts of love. Maybe we have to continue to highlight men having powerful and loving relationships with their daughters. Maybe we write *different* books. Maybe we work on ourselves and our assumptions. Does the joy then start here? Can the large ripples we want to see start from the smallest collective movements?

I want to showcase a particular path to joy in hopes that others can be inspired to carve their own. How can Black men celebrate and how do they celebrate? When I asked this question to Terrance Lee, he confided in me that no one had asked him that before. And although he shares that he is indeed proud of himself and what he's achieved, he knows there is work to do. "During that time of reflection, it does feel good to see areas where I've grown and accomplished things... a lot of my goals have to do with self-improvement/transformation. But I have to be honest, I don't think I really celebrate the way that I should." What if Black men were *incentivized* to celebrate? And I don't mean the champagne-popping images we see in music videos; I mean celebrating with positive self-talk, showing up for themselves, and feeling compelled to show who they are, even if that goes against the single story society has built for them.

On Instagram, I've been following a few Black male content creators who are openly sharing their self-care routines, and I am loving that! I see Black men spending time with their children and families, creating mini vlogs, taking pride in simple things like washing their faces, ironing their clothes—celebrating just being. So what does this mean for the era of young Black men coming up and taking space on these social media platforms? I think there's a huge opportunity to applaud these ways of existing, and this is as urgent as urgent gets. When I see Black men showing up and slowing down enough to begin intentionally building their own unique story for themselves, a little bit of hope trickles its way through my body. I take my role in this quite seriously. I go back to my core act of starting with the self. I have control over how I speak about the Black men in my life and how they've contributed to my own journey and success. This is my contribution: to continue to highlight the men who've shown me what it means to love. This is a thread I'm sure you've seen strengthened over the course of this book. Love. How can it not start there?

My brother takes care of the women in his life. He will check in on our mother, bring her groceries, and nudge her to exercise and move her body. This is one of the many quiet yet powerful traits that he carries with him always. As a young girl, I watched how caring and genuine he was with our mother, our aunts, and our grandmother, and this planted the seed that I too should be held from a place of love. He showed the women in our family love and kindness unconditionally. He showed me the effect of love and kindness. There was happiness in the way he connected with family and how he still continues to create a life for himself and his wife that feels authentic to his own living. I was proud of him. I am proud of him. I never told him that. We all show others love in different ways. Is it okay to love ourselves differently too?

I remember many small moments where I felt incredibly safe when my brother was by my side. Whether we were at the park playing baseball on a weekend when my cousin came to stay with us, or walking to the corner store to grab a bag of chips or a Coke, I had the strength of my brother to protect me. I can't say we were super close, but there was an unspoken understanding, a distant closeness. But even though this feeling of safety was indirect, I admired my brother in the way that he tended to steer clear of troublesome or problematic situations. That doesn't mean those dangers weren't there, but he was strong and clear about his dreams. Basketball was always important to him and he was dedicated to his art. I listened thoroughly to this. In my opinion, he is a nurturer. A natural caretaker. He taught me how to love.

The Black men in my life taught me that mentorship, coaching, and showing up for your community were invaluable. The how-to-show-up part has always looked different for me, but the coaching and mentorship was something I was born with, there's no denying that. Even when I couldn't find my place in my family, I squinted my eyes and I could still see the ripples of mentorship showing up and holding space.

I want to keep this dreaming fluid; I want it to flow like the longest of rivers. I want the world to pay attention to Black men and the gentle acts of loving that we witness—and showcase the heck out of it. All it takes is letting go of an old, single story that isn't serving anyone. *Can we dream?*

14

House Inspection: Coming Home

"The ache for home lives in all of us. The safe place where we can go as we are and not be questioned."

—Maya Angelou

When I look out of my small office window, I see half of a dying tree. The side of the tree that faces me has branches that are withered and sulking. The other half, which I cannot see from the window, is healthy and thriving. When I was a child, we moved so much I would not bother looking out the windows for fear of coming home one day to find the view had changed. Now, looking at this tree for what feels like hours, I consider its sides. How can two opposites exist together like this? How can life be so utterly close to the essence of death and still thrive? Does one side infect the other? Is that even the right word? Would a tree even look at itself the way we do? And if we have not yet found home within ourselves and we feel like all our unnourished parts are much too visible, is it still possible to find the thriving side?

What's fascinating to me is that all I have to do is make the choice to walk around to the lush side of the tree. I may not have a choice in the ways in which one side of the tree dies or folds in on itself, but I can ultimately control where I decide to stand and for how long. Just like I have the choice whether to latch on to a single story or investigate something different. In fact, this reminds me of the words of someone who's been in my ear throughout the evolution of this book. It was the one and only Maya Angelou who said, "If you don't like something, change it. If you can't change it, change your attitude."[6] There's some serious truth in that! Because really, our perspective can definitely *influence* the stories we tell about ourselves, the people we speak about, what we consume, and how we absorb it all. What I see and observe has weight. It is unique to me. Who else will be looking through these eyes, right? I can witness a death and a life at the same time, depending on where I choose to stand. Hmm.

But joy and living aren't one-dimensional. Maya Angelou speaks often about the art of living life in her book *Wouldn't Take Nothing for My Journey Now*, and it's had me thinking about the past, the present, and the future, and how the moments in between can also be filled with extreme pain. Pain that does not just go unnoticed. Even amongst all of the clarity that's started to surface along this pathway, I can tell that this past season has been a rough one. There were many hard truths to face, both inside of the smallness of an individual life and in the complexity of society as a whole. I had to prepare my muscles for the plethora of tough questions I'd have to ask myself, my family, and essentially the world. I had to be okay with tabling the questions I was not ready to ask my family.

Is there really space for joy and laughter amidst all of the turmoil of the world? Can we really dance, unearth our true selves, build communities, build wealth, and show up authentically while various Black communities across the world face so many inequities? Now is probably as good a time as any to check in with that one big unlearning that you wanted to focus on. *How close are you now? What do you need? It's okay if you don't know yet.* There is still room for joy.

This past winter taught me that we can let the joy seep in. Leaning into joy as soon as it arrives is a huge part of spreading that joy too. We deserve happiness right alongside that unsettling fear and uncertainty. I've said this from page one, but now I *feel* it, and that's the progress I want to revel in. And thanks to my many conversations with the Black leaders and the intuitiveness of my guides, I can map, track, and celebrate the acknowledgement that there's a difference here. I can build a home here. I look back, count all the steps I've taken this season, and become witness to my own evolution. This, my friends, is growth. I can see small movements forward and I can acknowledge and still celebrate the times where I fell backwards, the bruises on my backside a reminder that making mistakes can be a bridge to trying again. This was exactly what

I hoped this book would do for me, but what you take away is up to you. *Maybe take a few moments to consider your own expectations at this point.*

I'm thinking about the house I lived in for the last thirteen years. I can't help but admit that it was a place that I *called* home and watched my child grow up in, but it never really *felt* like home. And this is not because of its size, or the cosmetic deficiencies, or its hidden location in the city and the fact that any time someone asked where in Vancouver I lived and I said "Champlain Heights," no one knew where it was. What I've come to learn about my own joy as I've neared the end of this book is that I've been looking for home in the physical sense before I found it within myself.

This whole book, this journey, these conversations, the learning and unlearning were all in partnership with finding home and a sense of belonging inside of myself, and this is where it's supposed to start and where it will always continue. *Inside myself.* So maybe that is why this building of home is the last season. It's what this book has been doing this whole time, it's been bringing me home.

Insert breathing space here, friends.
I needed that. *What do you need right now?*

———

After some time had passed, I wrote the last part of this chapter in a small cafe down the street from my new home that I now own. I'll always reflect and think back to all the places I've been, but I don't miss the sight of that dying tree outside of my old window, even though I do think about it often. I wonder what's changed and what remains the same. Is it still thriving?

When my partner and I decided to take the leap and buy a house, we drove the two hours out from Vancouver to the building site in the small town of Harrison Hot Springs, BC, even though we knew there was nothing but dirt in the spot where the house would eventually stand.

The mortgage process was intense. Having to prove myself and secure a mortgage on just my income—an income that was uncertain, because in publishing and with a role I built for myself, *nothing* is guaranteed. But this interrogation of worthiness felt familiar. Heck, I've spent my whole life proving myself and demanding space in rooms not built for me. So moving and buying a house was not only a massive act of self-trust (I've never needed it more), it was also climbing over a major systemic barrier that I didn't even see until it was placed directly in front of me. In front of my family. I climbed over it with fear in my eyes. But it was important to take up space and hold it. To dream just a bit. To imagine.

Arriving at the plot of land, I stared at the possibility. I bent down and dug my fingers into the frozen dirt and clutched it just like I witnessed my younger self doing at the beginning of this book—remember, to start we have to look at the end. I glanced to my left and tilted my head as I pictured what my view would be like from my soon-to-be office. I thought about how, as the seasons pass, the mountains that stand high outside my large window will always be there. No one can take them, move them, or change them. There is safety in knowing. And although the seasons would shift and continue to cycle through their usual changes, they wouldn't fall. They wouldn't allow their environment to do the speaking for them.

I have been living in this new house for three nights and it already *feels* like home. There's a calmness around me that almost feels overwhelming, in a good way, likely because the gentle waters nearby feel like too tidy an ending, especially when I recall that the good in my life has always been shadowed by moments of darkness. That's something I have yet to let go of, that fear that something good in its purest form will at some point be whisked away from me before I can even raise my hands in protest.

I texted that old high school friend I spoke about in the spring to tell her about our new home. She was happy for me. She was never the one to suspect or wonder how someone like me who has spent a life of hard living could climb out from under it and emerge nourished and driven. My community helped me get here, yes, but without a journey into self-love and self-trust, I'd still be that scared, quiet girl letting people steal everything from me. I'd be just like the dying side of the tree outside of my old window. **Final moment to harvest: My love for myself was *always* there. I just had to dig it out. I had to nurture it.** Friends, this is huge. *Have you been tracking your own moments of harvest in your notebooks?*

When I think about my childhood best friend, I reflect on how our lives have changed over the past twenty years and how I am closer to embodying stability and love than I was all those years ago. It's reaffirming because it just goes to show that this work is ever-evolving, cyclical, and maybe never-ending. And writing this chapter while in winter, I can see the changing of the season just months away. The shift into a new cycle. I see a very different me this upcoming spring, with my hands in the dirt. I'll slow down enough to allow myself a moment or two to dream forward. I predict I'll be slowing down a lot more in the new year and every year after that, for that matter. I'll be asking some big questions of myself and redefining what home is and how that too can shapeshift with the seasons.

Just like the various phases of the moon guide the tide and the sun is connected to whether or not certain sea life can make oxygen to breathe, the seasons show us the temporariness of life—and I for one am paying close attention. I am beautifully haunted by Meghan Watson's words that "self-love is not urgent" and this is something that I almost need to tattoo on my body as a reminder, one that no one can take from me. The more I pay attention to the seasons and the world around me, the more I feel inspired to slow down. I must try my best to remember this when things feel too tough or when I want to quit this journey, which has happened multiple times during the drafting of this book.

I thought back to my Say No with Love workshop. This is what makes me feel at home, building tools for my community and watching them rise! Every time I've delivered this workshop, I've witnessed awakenings, revelations, and life-changing ripples. This is the power of turning the lens inward. Since the workshop's inception, I've been razor-focused on slowly, over time, peeling back the old layers of myself and examining the shedding. And maybe winter can be used for this task. I'm not sure why we tend to skip this work. It's foundational, we can learn so much from this investigation. It is here that we can surely be at home. *What does home feel like for you?*

Inspiring others to build their own definition of home within the self *before* looking at the outside influences has had major effects on my own daily life, right down to my first thoughts in the morning. No longer do I wake up pondering how I can best serve others today. Instead, I wake up and immediately assess my body. What does it need in this moment? I summon my heart and set an intention for how I want to move forward that day. How do I want to feel? I have control over this. I can't control whether or not the rain decides to pelt down on my head, whether or not the gas prices continue to rise, or whether or not one of my sisters is feeling the pain and heartache of a lost loved one. But I can indeed decide how I show up, because

I have control over this—over how I show up for myself (first) and then allow myself to check in with what I have to offer to my community today. Each day will be different. I meet myself where I am at. I am kind. Understanding. I tell myself it's okay to not be one hundred percent today. I tell myself I am capable of positively changing the lives of those around me. I can be my own mother. I can hold close the wisdom of my guides. I can smile at the wisdom of the Black leaders that I now hold and no one can ever take from me. I can hold myself safe.

I love sitting here at my computer in front of my massive window, and as people walk by, they look in, maybe in awe of my space and how it is uniquely mine. I never shut the blinds. I encourage people to look in. I want them to see me. I have nothing to hide here. Go ahead and form an opinion. Hold it tight if you need to. I've worked so hard for everything I have today. And even though that fear of home slipping through my fingers is always present, I can quiet it. I can remind myself of the winding road I followed to get here and claim the time to reflect on what it's taught me about myself, my community, and the wider world around me. This work I have done in finding and building home has strengthened my desire to break templates and not squeeze myself into the narrowness of someone's definition of me. Oh, I want to celebrate this!

I have to show appreciation to all the Black leaders I've been in conversation with. All who have indirectly spoken about their own desire for home within themselves. I don't think I ever would have come to this conclusion without them, without writing this book. I have learned so much over the last four seasons. It was James Baldwin who said, "Perhaps home is not a place but simply an irrevocable condition."[7] I've found home for myself after forty years of looking for it in the dirt.

And isn't that what we all want? *Can you articulate what it is that you want?*

My own definition of home has shapeshifted since youth and I do believe it will continue to morph. As I continue to build up the sense of self that has been missing for the majority of my life, I continue to witness the essence of my true self emerge. The more I speak to other marginalized creators, the more I feel connected to myself, closer to home.

But there has always been one constant that I am now coming to realize. Home, for me, is centred in safety, security, and feeling taken care of. Like I mentioned in the fall, this is not something I've ever had in my life, and the emotional realization that this was key for me was somewhat devastating. What if I could never find it? What if I did not deserve to feel safe and secure, whether financially, with the work I do, where I live, or who I live with? But again, it's that self-doubt that always seeps in no matter how much work I've done, or no matter what I've carried forward from a particular season.

At first, this journey was about me and my own personal path. That's true. But it's also about coming into contributions

I can offer my communities. And I say communities *plural* because it's impossible to expect to find nourishment for all the parts of the self through *one* community. The different parts of myself require different things, spaces, and people. Just like that dying tree. Its sun-facing side may need more water, the shaded side, a bit more warmth. We have to know ourselves to know what we need more of. And only then can we curl up within ourselves and declare that, finally, we are home.

Outside my window, after winter, I saw the cusp of spring again as the landscapers planted new trees, the hints that a new cycle of work is on its way. I sat in my small pink chair by the window and thought about this. How home is new life, growth. So much has changed since I inspected the dying side of the tree out front of my old house. Today, now, and in the future, there will be no uprooting. I walked over to my front door and placed the heavy cement mosaic my son made for me in kindergarten on the front step. I've had it all these years. I brought it home. The view of Bear Mountain grounds me. A student of mine once told me that she was suspicious of joy, and I think if I am to be honest, at first, we all are. But to begin the work of scaffolding a home inside of the first glimmer of joy requires such focus, and from that focus, joy.

Think about home if you can. How can you build for yourself a safe and authentic space to just be? I never would have imagined myself here, friends. There was a single story built for me too, but I turned away from it. I deserved more. We all do.

Winter *Un*learnings

LET'S UNLEARN:
DREAMS SHOULD ALWAYS BE OUT OF REACH.

Dreaming is a powerful way to picture yourself sitting inside the most concentrated piece of joy. But at some point, we have to walk toward it, or let it go. Dreams are meant to be realized. And if they can't be brought to fruition, then at least you can see your own footprints in the dirt. That journey counts too.

LET'S UNLEARN:
WE CAN'T CHANGE A HISTORY OR PATTERN OF STEREOTYPES.

The way in which we interact with a single story is the first step at creating new stories. How we respond to an unexpected gentle touch or an act of kindness dictates the next story that will be written. How we redefine the language we use with ourselves and for ourselves will do this same work.

LET'S UNLEARN:
HOME CAN ONLY BE A
PHYSICAL PLACE.

I feel like I don't have to unpack this any further!

LET'S UNLEARN:
OUR YOUNGER SELVES SHOULD
STAY IN THE PAST.

I find it interesting that this unlearning (looking back) came up again at the end of this winter cycle as it did in the spring. All the more proof that this work is cyclical. The past will always show up. Why should we shove it back down with asking, "What is this, really?" I know now that part of why my joy feels powerful enough to shine through the cracks has to do with how I stop and acknowledge past happenings. If that's my path, then that's my path. Maybe this is not safe work for others who cannot safely re-enter their pasts. So carve your own path, friends. Don't forget!

LET'S UNLEARN:
LOVE IS A NOUN.

My own language has guided me into an action. Love as a noun is connected to states of being, for sure, but love is a choice. We choose to show this or we do not. So when we start with ourselves as the recipients of this love, we get to filter it through all the parts of ourselves and we can direct it outwardly from there. When love feels out of reach or absent, that is the time in which we can reflect on how necessary loving is and remind ourselves of all the ways we've received love in the past and plan for its reimagined future.

How much closer are you to understanding your own joy? How have your own tools played a role?

Don't forget to revisit the cyclical questions from the community call to carry you forward:

- What do I need or want to make space for right now?
- How am I really feeling? I want to be honest about my feelings with myself and others.
- What feels heavy? I want to try to let go of this by season's end.

The Final Unlearning

We made it. Here we are at the end of the winter season, the end of a full cycle. I'm the same person, in the same body, but something has been unlocked. A part of myself that was not accessible before is completely available now. Not only do I feel like a different person than the one who first started this journey of joy-discovery, but I'm carrying a full bag of tools and resources to use for the next cycle. Check in with yourself now too. What's different? Maybe I'll lay them all out on our communal table just for a moment:

- using affirmations
- looking at myself in the mirror often
- paying close attention to the language I use with myself
- boundary-setting as a lifestyle
- aligning my priorities every year
- establishing my non-negotiables and saying no with love
- compiling my unlearnings and building a new home every year
- calling on guides
- rediscovering things that brought joy

- reimagining
- letting go
- discovering joy
- deep listening
- slowing down

I'm prepared to continue the lifelong work of bettering myself and helping out my community where I can. And that's the bit that I need folks to understand: that there is no end to building up a sense of self. There is no end to loving the self. There is no end to joy-discovery. Your tools may change every cycle, too, but old tools will inform the new tools.

When I spoke about loving and living over the past year, whether that was with the Black leaders, or with family and close friends, we could all agree on the same visual: that this work moves in circles that overlap experiences, learnings, and mistakes. Relationships also re-emerge. It's up to us to slow down enough to appreciate the learnings (and unlearnings) each season. I used to zoom by life trying desperately to keep up with those around me, and, friends, that is exactly what was keeping joy from me. I remember watching the movie *Pursuit of Happyness*, a film starring Will Smith based on the true story of Chris Gardner, who went from being homeless for a year to working full time as an elite stockbroker. There was a scene during Chris's six-month unpaid internship (he's competing with twenty privileged candidates for a coveted full-time position at the firm) where, in order to stay competitive with his colleagues, he had to find ways to shave off seconds from the work he did making calls to potential clients. Instead of wasting time hanging up the phone and picking it up to make his next call, he would simply press the hang-up button, the receiver still firmly held in his hand. This saved him time. I think about that often. It was emotional because I could relate. Back in those old burnout days, I would skip drinking water to save myself having to walk to the sink during work. I wanted to keep up. I wanted to do a good job. Those seconds matter to folks like us who always seem to be behind everyone else just because that's where we always had to start. Behind.

Even as I typed this, I caught myself glancing at the clock. Even through all of the unlearning this cycle, the old ways of living do not just disappear, y'all, no matter how much work we've done. But the amount of time I spend inside the fear of falling behind has shrunk, and that's what I have to pay attention to because that is growth. I want you to look back at that growth too. Every time I look at that clock I take a long breath. Slow inhale, hold, slow and forceful breath out. I know I need time to appreciate being inside of the moment. Cliché as it sounds, no one is guaranteed a tomorrow, and I think we often forget that. Part of my commitment to living my best life is to be undeniably present as much as possible. This is where existing turns into living.

In late spring, I took a mindful walk through the Bridle Trail in Harrison, BC. Looking around, it was as if someone had picked me up and plopped me down in a lush jungle. It was so different from the previous season. Ferns were sprouting everywhere, and there were more shades of green than I had ever seen in my life. I saw so many trees, perhaps tired in their age, cut down and lying on their sides with their many inner rings exposed. The smell of chipped cedar tunnelled through me. But those cut trees, it was their rings that told a story. Each ring represented a year of growth. No more than a sliver. But the growth was there. I traced my fingers over the circles. I thought about what could have been accomplished in a year and what likely had to be pushed forward. With this big cedar lying flat on its side, I could see its past. I could see its journey and evidence of living.

Even though I can't *see* my own evidence or proof of living, and I don't want anyone to have to cut me open to see it, I know it's there. Every small push forward each season leads me closer to my own happiness inside of my own well-defined living and loving. Through this work of joy-discovery, I've learned that joy is something to be unearthed, not necessarily sought out. And there's a big difference. Can you see it? Is this the biggest unlearning? Let's remove the problem of not knowing where to look and take it off the table. We are left with the monumental yet more accessible task of slowly and carefully removing life's weight from our shoulders, one layer at a time. Offloading, releasing, unlearning, dropping off, saying no, slowing down, listening deep, and calling in community . . . This is part of that unearthing. I shared this observation with a small group of writer friends, and there was a mutual understanding or energy in the room. It all started to make sense.

———

My belief systems changed this past cycle. I started to view the world in a different way because I was essentially rewiring my brain. This evolution, this growth, isn't static. I will shapeshift fluidly depending on the season, and all of these various selves combined make up the unique and complex self. The qualities I used to want to hide, like the quiet attention, the desire to be listened to, the difficulty discussing identity tropes, are all pieces of me that I want to explore for life. I'm calling those pieces into the room too. This mindset shift is major, friends. This discovery is monumental. I have massive gratitude for this. And it is this same feeling, ultimately, that I want for my communities—the understanding that we can change and grow, celebrate and love, all while experiencing pain. I am not here to solve anything. I am here to share, to flourish, to stumble, to be frustrated, and to pull myself forward. And to make space for this, I've had to release and let go. I've had to unlearn these things:

- Looking back is a negative thing.
- Happiness can *only* form at the beginning of an experience.
- I have to love my body all the time.
- We don't deserve second chances.
- Sisterhood as a singular experience.
- Familial love is unconditional.
- Happiness can't exist inside of tumultuous times.
- Being loud = being heard.

- Self-love should be immediate and linear.
- Fitting a mould = belonging.
- There are easy answers to identity conversations.
- Everything can be solved in a single season.
- Survival mode is the same as thriving.
- Dreams should always be out of reach.
- We can't change a history or pattern of stereotypes.
- Home can only be a physical place.
- Our younger selves should stay in the past.
- Love is a noun.
- Joy has to be sought out.

Can you let it all go?

Now that I have summarized my own unlearnings, I can make space for *new* learnings and wisdom from my community and my guides, which is something that will happen every cycle, for the rest of my life. I've made mistakes and they have been acknowledged and reflected on. I have to promise myself to keep this up as a consistent practice. I have to! *Can y'all commit to that too?* I have a process now. I have an overflowing toolkit of support, love, and how-tos.

I will likely never be completely free from financial woes, physical pain in my body, or imperfect relationships, and let's be real, I will never have all the answers. I will continue to make mistakes and say yes to things I should have run far away from, but the difference now is that I can look at all of it and know that it doesn't make me less of a person, less Black, or less happy. My joy, y'all, will stem from every part of me, and I deserve time inside every piece when it shows itself. I want the same for my community. This book is meant to be a reminder of the work I've done and how I'll have to work my mindset muscle on the daily to continue this work. Don't forget the work you've done to get here. You are part of this discovery too.

But let's get back to celebrating! We are here, y'all!

And having planted the seeds, helped them grow, harvested the crops, and weathered the gusts of winter winds it's time to spread out the bounty on the table and sit down with the community to enjoy the seasons' gifts. I can look back now at all the seeds planted and pushed into the brilliant earth, the weeds pulled and discarded, and the slow growth in certain areas, acknowledged and tended to. The conditions are right for another cycle, but my hands are tired and dry from the dirt. Time to nourish. My body needs it.

Over the past few weeks, I had a lot of scary health issues that I felt derailed me, set me back. I had a hard time focusing on writing a book about joy when my world felt so tipped over. My days were riddled with stress and anxiety and, worst of all, fear that I was imagining everything that was happening to me. I almost thought of emailing my editor to say . . . I think I may need a lot more time. But then something interesting happened. I started to recall my conversations with the Black leaders. I was reminded that I had new tools and ways to work through difficulties, and that, yes, I could still focus on joy in moments of extreme difficulty. There will never be a "perfect" time for anything.

Let's call everyone into the room and exchange gratitude. It's time to look at the harvest:

- Take the time to slow down. To just ... think.
- I am so grateful to have access to books, writers, mentors, teachers, and other people's inspirational experiences; it's a massive contributor to my joy.
- Joy is connected to making mistakes.
- I need to invest in myself early.
- Learning to love yourself is learning to let go of who you thought you should be.
- That is not what shaped me.
- Asking is not always as easy as just pushing the words out.
- We have to expose the narratives that cause us to second-guess our paths. Can we reimagine where we want to go?
- Joy starts at home. It starts with the self.
- My love for myself was *always* there. I just had to dig it out. I had to nurture it.

The purpose of this book has shifted as I wrote it. It became less about who the leaders I spoke to were and more about how what they shared with me allowed me to unlearn all the restraints and negative thoughts—the unvalidated belief systems have held me back. And this book allowed me to let those things go. That is the difference between this book and any other that I've read. Maybe you, my readers, are not here to learn but to unlearn. To let go too. I am so grateful for everyone who said yes to this work of letting go.

Our celebration is long overdue. I want now to thank the leaders and my guides. Individually. I want to call everyone onto this page and thank them for helping me get ready for the next cycle in this journey to joy and self-love. I wanted to give up many times along this journey. But I am happy to say I am still here.

Alex Elle helped me to unchain myself from the limitations of living. I am so much closer to my authentic self because of her. My past does not and will not define who I am or who the world thinks I should be. When I speak my truths, the world will either support me or not. Alex taught me that my own essence and living doesn't have to be started from birth. As an adult, I can give myself the parent I so desperately wanted as a child. I can be my own mother.

Even with this new set of tools I gained from Alex, I still hold on to a lot of shame. Shame about who I was and how I grew up. The shame seemed unclouded. Incredibly visible. It still does and likely always will. But I offer a big hug of gratitude to Ifrah Ahmed, who reminded me that it's never too late to start something, to build my own traditions. We can all build our own traditions.

235

I don't have to have traditional relationships with other Black women to feel whole. I still feel seen when I think about the conversation with Téa Mutonji. Thank you, girl.

Look at this bounty! It's pretty damn amazing to know and to feel like the one personality trait that held me back for forty years is now my superpower. I have Keni Domiguez and Terrance Lee to thank for showing me the way to use my deep-listening skills as a groundbreaking tool. I just might be writing another book on that topic, y'all. Talk about a gift. Thank you.

But that's not all. Let's go back to the very beginning of this cycle. Let's go back to where we started. Let's speak to the body. I can love my body and *not* love my body at the same time. This vessel that carries me allows me to do the work that I love; this body almost tried to kill me, but my gut instinct told me to speak up for it and at the same time listen to it. No one knows my body the way I do. No medical professional can take that. I won't let them. Cicely Belle Blain is someone who showed me that the body is sacred. We have control over what we allow into our bodies and with whom we allow close and intimate contact. I know this will resonate with so many of you.

We are complex beings, but we don't have to have all the answers. David Chariandy changed the trajectory of my identity journey forever. He reminded me of the danger of race because it has always been this restrictive category that was imposed upon us. But we can find our way. As David told me during our beautiful conversation, "We have articulated it anew and we found more in it than those who have aimed the idea at us. But in order for it to do that work of attending to our complexities and our liberation from these categories and restrictions, it has to keep being complex." Yes! This conversation connected to race has to be more than what we automatically think it is. When David heard me talk about ordinary life and how I live it, he told me that this is where Blackness is being articulated in its most interesting and complex ways. This is living.

Anais Granfosky was someone whom I watched on TV, someone I admired from youth. Knowing nothing about her life or her past or her relationship to her mother, I admired her movements. Talking to her and feeling a huge sense of freedom in connecting over the complex relationships we've both had with our mothers—the biggest unlearning—released me. Joy can be linked to mistakes and failure as mothers and daughters.

Meghan Watson has gifted me the biggest step toward self-love and joy. I didn't expect this going in, but I now know that slowing down was the biggest thing I was denying myself, out of fear. I am changing that and it's seeping into everything I do. Even if we rush through things out of fear of being left behind in this incredibly fast-paced world, the shifting seasons will do their thing regardless. So why can't we move in the way the seasons do?

But with all of this growth, releasing, and unlearning, there are still mistakes that I have to hold on to and this is okay. At least for now. I recall the tree lying on its side with its rings of living exposed for everyone to see. There were seasons of rot, of going backwards, of growth unravelling too.

This book is a communal offering, something that allows us to ditch the idea of the singular Black experience because that holds us back. The more I share my experience and learnings, the more I hope others will share their stories of living and loving so that we can see so many different ways toward joy. This is a feeling and a hope I can't deny.

My own story and journey are a small drop in the bucket when we consider the vast living and loving experiences of Black folks all over the world. There is no one single experience, there is no template, no one single way to call joy in (thank goodness for that). The complexity of our individual daily lives can be found inside the simple act of existing within our most current and most authentic selves. Is that not the best way to show up for joy, even amidst the everyday difficulties? And sure, we didn't cover everything, but that's the point. We can take what we didn't get done and make a plan to prepare for the next cycle.

So this is a celebration. This is a place where we can all come together in whatever shape or form we currently find ourselves, and we apologize for nothing. Turn the music up. Do something for yourself, because the act of slowing down enough to give yourself what you need is part of the gift. I know this now. We can show up here to breathe and to hold space for the future selves that we deserve to meet and spend the rest of our lives getting to know. We deserve that. I feel like I've said that a lot in this book, but it's true. I deserve full control over my small but flourishing garden. We deserve to push through that soil as our roots secure us in place. We deserve to let our leaves unfurl and petals blossom as slowly as we need them to. We deserve to thrive.

We need to slow down and take breaks from our lives too. Sometimes we need to forget who we are in order to come back to ourselves whole. I pass the mic to the most influential guide in my life, Maya Angelou: "When I return home, I am always surprised to find some questions I sought to evade had been answered and some entanglements I had hoped to flee had become unraveled in my absence."[1]

Coming Full Circle

"It was love's absence that let me know
how much love mattered."
—bell hooks

Y'all, I've been looking for love my whole life, and like
bell hooks, I found myself drowning in nothingness
without its presence. That's pretty hard to admit, and I
didn't realize this until reaching the end. Until I started to slow
down and ask, "What is this, really?" Every seemingly wrong
decision or negative encounter, all the relationships where I
let people take pieces of me over and over, was a search for
love. I was searching for love elsewhere, having no idea that
it existed inside my own body and that I could control how it
spilled out or how it didn't. I could curate who I let experience
it with me, or who didn't deserve a seat at the table. Love is a
movement, an action. Love is ever present. Love is feeling safe.
Joy and love are intertwined.

In my novel, *Junie*, I wrote about love. In fact, the entire narrative follows the main character's quest for it, buried within herself. She questions love. She asks the world about the colour of love, the weight of it, the un-steal-ability of it. She clutches love in her young fist and refuses to let anyone take from her what she has finally given herself. I think about Junie now, how she trusted the Rose of Sharon bush outside her window and how she knew, instinctively, that nothing could break its spirit or stop its growth. She saw the same tree I saw outside my window, except Junie first noticed the living, where I focused on the dying. When I think about my reason for writing that novel, maybe it was just another letter to you. Or, as I mentioned before, maybe it was a song with the lyrics I just instinctively knew.

But let's keep talking about love. Because chances are, it's not and hasn't ever been a comfortable conversation for us. It's never been soft or attached to the self. Love was always framed as something we find from some other source. It's okay if we looked for it within the pages of books. We looked for it in music. We likely turned up the volume on our favourite song. We listened to it over and over. We may have noticed people on the bus, men with their arms flung around some woman. How that same woman peered out the bus window, dazed, watching the world zoom past. Maybe she was looking for love too.

After the first leg of this journey, I can confirm that, for me, right now, love is safety. Love is feeling safe enough to re-soften even the hardest edges of myself that have been formed after years of upheaval and neglect. bell hooks says, "Love and abuse cannot coexist."[1] If we don't love ourselves as defined by us, what does that say about how we treat ourselves?

What about the absence of love?

When teaching creative writing, I tell my students to consider the absence in their writing. To give voice to what isn't there, what was never there, or what was left behind through loss. I ask them to look back, reflect. For the most part, they get it and they see the value. But there's always one student who questions the purpose of looking back. We really have to let ourselves call this in as routine. For me, the constant reminders of what could have been or what used to be poke pin holes through my heart. I tell you this now because you likely won't be able to locate the source of such pain when you feel it, when it takes over you. You will make assumptions and create stories about why you are to blame for lack of love or for full not knowing where to find, grab it, hold on to it. Love and joy coexist.

I could list all the tangible things I did not have as a young girl. The absence of these things is a weight to carry, but it is not as heavy now that I can see the unrefined love head-on, see the crest of it on the horizon. There were many opportunities for explosions of love. But what we can look back on now, and maybe if we are lucky take comfort in it, is maybe those who denied us love just didn't know how to love. Maybe they felt dismissed in their own youth. What are the patterns of living and loving that you need to break?

———

Throughout this book I've shared openly that I believe everything, including joy and love, start with and from the self. Why is it that we are so darn eager to find love, joy, and acceptance, externally? Learning more about how much we have to rewire ourselves in order to come up with an authentic aura, or way of living, loving, and laughing, I can see (finally) that it is sorta up to me to make myself happy. Anything else from anyone else is just extra. And so, it's up to you as well.

The ways we love and don't love ourselves can be private too. Putting my journey into a book was a big decision for me, but because I process my own emotions through writing, this was an intrinsic way for me to work. Your documentation may be different.

Remember, I am not here to warn you or to teach you how to do anything. We can press rewind on movies all we want, but in life, we don't get to do that. Now I can say that I am here to guide, to ask what if, to predict. It's my hope that you pay attention to what the world around you is trying to say. I'll continue to try to make that as evident as I can. Maybe I'll show up as a harder-than-usual gust of wind or a sudden downpour of rain. Maybe you'll feel me as the scorching sun, pushing the clouds apart. When you slow down and look up at the sky's offering, it's in these moments that you can find love. You can fill the absence that, for now, you cannot explain.

We have tools. We have worked through some complex things this past year, and you know what? We are stronger for it. But this strength is not something we have to use or fall on. And we don't have to be strong all the damn time. We can have strength and need help at the same moment. We can have strength and feel waves of great pain. We can have strength and still need someone to lovingly run the palm of their steady hand down our back. Promise me you won't forget that.

In today's world, it feels as though love and desire are interchangeable. All I want to say here is that they are not. When we figure out what love actually looks like for us, we see, with clarity, how to exist inside of love and we know exactly what to hold on to. What to protect. This is the part we forget to consider. How do we move, think, and exist when love is around us, especially when it feels foreign? When I didn't have love, I watched the parts of myself that I didn't like begin to emerge. In relationships where I felt love was not defined or present, or where I confused love with lust and desire, I became angry, short-tempered, even vindictive. This hurt me when I looked in the mirror, and that's why that mirror exercise was so hard for me, each and every season.

But it wasn't me, it was the unbalanced combined chemistry of two people who just did not align or connect in all the ways needed for love to fully flex. This is what I started to pay attention to. To find and be immersed in love, I need to uncover the parts of myself that were (and maybe still are) buried under the weight of a lifetime of hard living. I need to bring them to the surface and nurture them. And I need to surround myself with people who can see those pieces and desire a connection with them. I need to exist inside an environment conditioned and built for loving.

I thank goodness for all of the guides in my ear the whole

way. I guess when you feel alone or inside the biggest absence of love, you can still call upon your sisters. Don't forget that either. I feel like I have been quoting Ms. Maya Angelou, bell hooks, and others throughout this book: they are always there, always ready to remind me of some wisdom I forgot I had access to.

We've done some serious work. We've challenged perceptions and assumptions. We've spoken up for what we need. We've said no to ridiculous asks and we've excavated a space for a joy so unique, it sits there, cradled and glowing.

With the first full cycle complete, I'm back to see that you still have your hands planted firmly in that dirt, but now, you are harvesting. Look at you, thinking about your future.

Reminders and signals will show themselves season after season. Slow down and pay attention. When you pull your hands from the dirt or slow down long enough to notice a tree lying on its side in some lush paradise, don't forget to trace your fingers down the rings of growth that maybe, for now, only you can see.

Look closely.

What legacy do you want to leave behind?

Folks often ask me why I wanted to work in publishing, an

industry that seems steeped in the past, a space where change shows itself in slow, small scoots forward; an industry that hardly pays me and where not everyone is welcomed to a seat at the table and where, even if they don't admit it, everyone is tired.

While working on this early this morning, I cracked wide open the biggest discovery ever about myself as a writer, as a Black woman, and as a champion of other writers.

Who better to share that with, than you? Here it is: When we create something and usher it out into the world, we give a part of ourselves away. A part we can't ever get back. I don't think folks (who don't create) understand the weight of that.

But there's an unexcavated love embedded in the work of championing the writers whose work I believe in. I can't do this work lightly, and I don't.

bell hooks said, "If our society had a commonly held understanding of the meaning of love, the act of loving would not be so mystifying."[2]

Doing this work, for me anyway, is an act of loving. An act that now takes place inside an exquisitely constructed home built specifically for the unique discovery of my own joy. Look back at everything you've let go of. I hope your definition of joy has grown and that you are ready to harvest every last piece of it.

Gratitude for My Guides and My Readers

It's important to acknowledge the physical and emotional work that went into compiling this book. This work was a generous offering from everyone I was in conversation with. I have so much love for the Black leaders who sat down with me for hours to share their stories and experiences with joy and in defining self-love. Not only did their experiences help to fill these pages with vivid and lush moments, but they helped me to define what has shaped me over the course of my life, including my relationships with my family and my own identity. Every conversation gave me hope for the future and validated the notion that this journey into self-love is one without an end.

To all the beautiful souls I have been in conversation with: Thank you, Alex Elle, Anais Granofsky, Cicely Belle Blain, David Chariandy, Ifrah Ahmed, Kenitra Dominguez, Meghan Watson, Téa Mutonji, Shakura S'Aida, and Terrance Lee. I felt in community with you folks and will forever push my gratitude out into the world as much as I can. Thank you to the guides who showed up unexpectedly and yet at the right time: Shakura S'Aida, that's you. I feel so much gratitude for my friends Wanda Taylor and Danielle Jernigan. We met through writing and bonded through a desire to build out the conditions to continue doing it. Thank you, friends.

This book has allowed me to investigate and fall into my own identity and find solace in the ever-evolving journey of self-love and joy, while acknowledging the fact that this is lifelong work. I have to say that there were so many people I wanted to be in conversation with, but whom I just didn't get a chance to talk to, so maybe that's work for another season. Remember, we can't do this work all at once. There are other Black leaders who were suggested to me, by my editors and other folks reading early versions of this book, but I either didn't feel compelled to reach out or maybe wasn't ready to. It's important for me to share that with all of you because much of this book was driven by the engine of gut instinct and heart. Shaping this book in a way that felt right for me is probably the biggest act of self-love and joy. It's growth I can try to track, but all the tree's branches are too far and wide to reach—and that's a good thing.

Thank you to the readers for taking this journey with me.

Let's take one last breath together.

Here we are at the end and also at the beginning. There is no single "Black experience" and there is no one way into joy. There are many nuanced folds, nooks, and turns on this long and winding path to joy. There is so much to let go of. This is the hardest part, especially because there is no end point to discovering what self-love feels like. This work moves in cycles that should continue as we change and grow with the shifting of each and every season.

Acknowledgements

After I submitted the final draft of this book, I took a three-day train ride across eight states, and more specifically through Mississippi, on my way to New Orleans, Louisiana, where I stayed for two weeks. It was Patricia Smith's book *Blood Dazzler* (my favourite book of poetry) that called me to New Orleans.

As the train entered and exited all of these beautiful places, my tiny train window framed each city like a painting. For two weeks, I was unable to understand why I felt such an emotional connection to being in these places I'd never been before. I later realized that many of the writerly guides in this book had ties to Mississippi, and I took my emotional reaction as a sign that I was right where I was supposed to be and for the right amount of time. Thank you to all the writerly legends who've whispered in my ear throughout the creation of this book.

ACKNOWLEDGEMENTS

I am beyond thrilled with how *Let It Go* has evolved. In the beginning, I didn't know what I wanted it to be, and I'll be honest, at first I was writing what I thought folks wanted me to write. But when I trusted myself enough to let that go, magic happened. Joy showed up. After multiple drafts, I noticed my true voice showing up on the page, and so I am so grateful to Jennifer Lambert and team HarperCollins Canada for helping me let go of the fear and just write in the way my heart wanted to. Much gratitude and respect to writers Jónína Kirton and Charlene Carr, who read the messy first draft. Your honesty and insights played a huge role in the final draft of this book.

To Aeman Ansari, who first commissioned me for this book! I know it's likely different than you had first envisioned, but without you, there would be no *Let It Go*. Thank you for the opportunity. And to my agent Sam Haywood, who always makes me feel like I can do anything in this publishing world; I thank you too.

I want to thank my family for the quiet encouragement that indirectly allowed me to hold the space I needed to write this book and all the books that came before it. Dad, Oliver, Richard, Mom, Auntie Virg, my brother David, and everyone else who never questioned my desire to do difficult things.

Thank you all for helping me find and hug my joy.

I'll never forget the big "Thriving vs Surviving" event we did, Wanda and Danielle! Thank you for that big boost of energy.

I've thanked all the amazing Black community leaders throughout this book and I'll save the final breath for y'all: Sharing conversations with you and learning from you has been a life-changing experience. Alex Elle, Anais Granofsky, Cicely Belle Blain, David Chariandy, Ifrah Ahmed, Kenitra Dominguez, Meghan Watson, Téa Mutonji, Shakura S'Aida, and Terrance Lee, Thank you!

Notes

SPRING COMMUNITY CALL: AFFIRMATIONS

Part epigraph: Sonya Renee Taylor, *The Body Is Not an Apology* (Oakland: Berrett-Koehler Publishers, 2018, 2021), 13.

1   Maya Angelou, *Wouldn't Take Nothing for My Journey Now* (New York: Random House, 1993), 56.

2   Sonya Renee Taylor, *The Body Is Not an Apology* (Oakland: Berrett-Koehler Publishers, 2018, 2021), 13.

3   Janice Gassam Asare, "What Is Fetishization and How Does It Contribute to Racism?" *Forbes*, February 7, 2021, https://www.forbes.com/sites/janicegassam/2021/02/07 /what-is-fetishization-and-how-does-it-contribute-to -racism/?sh=5b24e3fb6e39.

4   Hermione Hoby, "Toni Morrison: 'I'm Writing for Black People… I Don't Have to Apologise,'" *The Guardian*, April 25, 2015, https://www.theguardian.com/books/2015/apr/25/toni-morrison -books-interview-god-help-the-child.

5   Sonya Renee Taylor, *The Body Is Not an Apology*, 19.

6   Hadiya Roderique, "The Case for Black Joy," *FASHION*, February 1, 2019, https://fashionmagazine.com/flare/the-case -for-black-joy/.

7   Ifrah Ahmed, "A Somali-style Afternoon Break for Tea and Sweets Will Soothe the Spirit," *The Washington Post*, October 29, 2021, https://www.washingtonpost.com/food/2021/10/29 /somali-tea-break-bur-shaah-recipes/.

8   Suzanne Cope, publisher's book synopsis for *Power Hungry: Women of the Black Panther Party and Freedom Summer and Their Fight to Feed a Movement* (Penguin Random House, 2021), https://www.penguinrandomhouse.ca/books/706279 /power-hungry-by-suzanne-cope/9780593559147.

9   Rachel Montañez, "Here's How to Actually Help Women of Color with Burnout," *Forbes*, February 21, 2021, https://www .forbes.com/sites/rachelmontanez/2021/02/21/heres -how-to-actually-help-women-of-color-with-burnout /?sh=59ae0eb51167.

10 Glory Edim, *Well-Read Black Girl: Finding Our Stories, Discovering Ourselves* (New York: Ballantine Books, 2018), xiv.

SUMMER COMMUNITY CALL: REVISING OLD LANGUAGE

Part epigraph: Michelle Obama, ABC News interview with David Muir, 2017.

1   D'Shonda Brown, "The Meaning of Sisterhood for Black Women," *Essence*, updated June 16, 2021, https://www .essence.com/entertainment/the-meaning-of-sisterhood -for-black-women/.

2   bell hooks, *All About Love: New Visions* (New York: William Morrow and Company, 2021), 46.

3   James Baldwin, *The Fire Next Time* (New York: Vintage International, 1993), 27. First published 1963 by the Dial Press.

4   Angelou, *Wouldn't Take Nothing for My Journey Now*, 92.

5   Amanda Enayati, "The Importance of Belonging," CNN Health, June 1, 2012, https://www.cnn.com/2012/06/01/health/enayati-importance-of-belonging/index.html.

6   Anjelica Tejada, "Enough Is Enough, Give Black TikTok Creators the Recognition They Deserve," *The Ticker*, April 15, 2021, https://theticker.org/3577/opinions/enough-is-enough-give-black-tiktok-creators-the-recognition-they-deserve.

7   Ian Williams, *Disorientation: Being Black in the World* (Toronto: Random House Canada, 2021) 6.

8   Jennifer Granneman, "For Extroverts: 15 Ways to Be a Better Parent to Your Introverted Kid," Susan Cain, n.d., https://quietrev.com/15-ways-to-parent.

9   Marti Olsen Laney, *The Hidden Gifts of the Introverted Child* (Workman Publishing Company, 2005), 72.

10 Brianna Holt, "What They Mean When They Say You're 'Not Social Enough' at Work," *Zora Medium*, January 28, 2021, https://zora.medium.com/black-women-dont-have-the-freedom-to-be-introverts-at-work-ed17fd795aee.

FALL COMMUNITY CALL: ESTABLISHING NON-NEGOTIABLES

Part epigraph: Oprah Winfrey, commencement address to Wellesley College, May 30, 1997.

1   hooks, *All About Love*, 140.

2   Charlie Bloom and Linda Bloom, "Self-Trust and How to Build It," *Psychology Today*, September 12, 2019, https://www.psychologytoday.com/ca/blog/stronger-the-broken-places/201909/self-trust-and-how-build-it.

3   Janice Gassam Asare, "Understanding the White Gaze and How It Impacts Your Workplace," *Forbes*, December 28, 2021, https://www.forbes.com/sites/janicegassam/2021/12/28/understanding-the-white-gaze-and-how-it-impacts-your-workplace/?sh=6d7312764cd6.

4   George Elliott Clarke, *Whylah Falls* (Polestar Book Publishers, 2000).

5   Mark McConville, *Failure to Launch: Why Your Twentysomething Hasn't Grown Up Yet… and What to Do About It* (New York: G.P. Putnam's Sons, 2020), 18–19.

6   Jamaica Kincaid, *The Autobiography of My Mother* (New York: Plume, 1997), 97.

7   Krissah Thompson, "We Asked Black Mothers How They Find Their Joy. This Is What They Said," *The Washington Post*, September 20, 2019, https://www.washingtonpost.com/lifestyle/2019/09/20/we-asked-black-mothers-how-they-find-their-joy-this-is-what-they-said.

8   Lewis, Shantrelle, dir. *In Our Mothers' Gardens*, Array Releasing, 2021.

WINTER COMMUNITY CALL: BUILDING A DREAM HOME

Part epigraph: Paris Alexandra, "5 Ways I'm Centering My Black Joy and Protecting My Peace," *Self*, July 9, 2020, https://www.self.com/story/centering-black-joy-and-peace.

1 Hadiya Roderique, "Black on Bay Street: Hadiya Roderique Had It All. But Still Could Not Fit In," *The Globe and Mail*, November 4, 2017, updated February 22, 2023, https://www .theglobeandmail.com/news/toronto/hadiya-roderique -black-on-bay-street/article36823806.

2 Ashley Pointer, "Trap Music: Where It Came from and Where It's Going," Take Note: Inspiration for Music Makers, https://online.berklee.edu/takenote/trap-music-where -it-came-from-and-where-its-going.

3 Chimamanda N. Adichie, "The Danger of a Single Story," TEDGlobal 2009, https://www.ted.com/talks/chimamanda _ngozi_adichie_the_danger_of_a_single_story?language=en.

4 Prince Shakur, "Frank Ocean, *Moonlight*, and the New Era of Queer Black Men in Pop Culture," *Teen Vogue*, March 26, 2019, https://www.teenvogue.com/story/new-era-queer-black-men -pop-culture.

5 Andre M. Perry, "Black Men Have a Masculinity Problem and It's Hurting Their Kids' Sexual Health," *The Washington Post*, October 8, 2014, https://www.washingtonpost.com /posteverything/wp/2014/10/08/how-dads-are-ruining black-teens-sexual-health.

Chapter 14 epigraph: Maya Angelou, *All God's Children Need Traveling Shoes* (New York: Random House, 1986).

6 "Maya Angelou: In Her Own words" (BBC News, May 28, 2014), https://www.bbc.com/news/world-us-canada-27610770.

7 James Baldwin, *Giovanni's Room* (Vintage Books, 2013), 92. First published 1956 by the Dial Press.

THE FINAL UNLEARNING

1   Angelou, *Wouldn't Take Nothing for My Journey Now*, 139.

COMING FULL CIRCLE

Chapter epigraph: bell hooks, *All About Love: New Visions* (New York: William Morrow and Company, 2021).

1   hooks, *All About Love*, 6.

2   hooks, *All About Love*, 3.

Sources

Adichie, Chimamanda N. "Chimamanda Ngozi Adichie: The Danger of a Single Story." TEDGlobal 2009. https://www.ted.com/talks/chimamanda_ngozi_adichie_the _danger_of_a_single_story?language=en.

Ahmed, Ifrah F. "Somali-style Bur and Shaah Recipes to Soothe the Spirit." *The Washington Post*, October 29. 2021. https://www.washingtonpost.com/food/2021/10/29 /somali-tea-break-bur-shaah-recipes/.

Angelou, Maya. *All God's Children Need Traveling Shoes*. New York: Random House, 1986.

Asare, Janice Gassam. "Overcoming the Angry Black Woman Stereotype." *Forbes*, May 31, 2019. https://www.forbes .com/sites/janicegassam/2019/05/31/overcoming-the -angry-black-woman-stereotype/?sh=4a6a3bdc1fce.

Asare, Janice Gassam. "Understanding the White Gaze and How It Impacts Your Workplace." *Forbes*, December 28, 2021. https://www.forbes.com/sites/janicegassam/2021 /12/28/understanding-the-white-gaze-and-how-it-impacts -your-workplace/?sh=6d7312764cd6.

Asare, Janice Gassam. "What Is Fetishization and How Does It Contribute to Racism?" *Forbes*, February 7, 2021. https://www.forbes.com/sites/janicegassam/2021/02/07 /what-is-fetishization-and-how-does-it-contribute-to -racism/?sh=5b24e3fb6e39.

Bloom, Charlie and Linda Bloom. "Self-Trust and How to Build It." *Psychology Today*, September 12, 2019. https://www .psychologytoday.com/ca/blog/stronger-the-broken-places /201909/self-trust-and-how-build-it.

Brown, D'Shonda. "The Meaning of Sisterhood for Black Women." *Essence*, updated June 16, 2021. https://www.essence.com /entertainment/the-meaning-of-sisterhood-for-black-women.

Compton, Wayde. *After Canaan: Essays on Race, Writing, and Region*. Arsenal Pulp Press, 2021.

Cope, Suzanne. *Power Hungry: Women of the Black Panther Party and Freedom Summer and Their Fight to Feed a Movement*. Chicago: Chicago Review Press, 2022.

Edim, Glory. *Well-Read Black Girl: Finding Our Stories, Discovering Ourselves*. New York: Ballantine Books, 2018.

Enayati, Amanda. "The importance of belonging." CNN Health, June 1, 2012. https://www.cnn.com/2012/06/01 /health/enayati-importance-of-belonging/index.html.

Geronimus, Arline T. et al. "Do US Black Women Experience Stress-Related Accelerated Biological Aging? A Novel Theory and First Population-Based Test of Black-White Differences in Telomere Length." National Center for Biotechnology Information, March 10, 2010. https://www .ncbi.nlm.nih.gov/pmc/articles/PMC2861506.

Granneman, Jennifer. "For Extroverts: 15 Ways to Be a Better Parent to Your Introverted Kid." Susan Cain, n.d. https://quietrev.com/15-ways-to-parent.

Hoby, Hermione. "Toni Morrison: 'I'm Writing for Black People . . . I Don't Have to Apologise.'" *The Guardian*, April 25, 2105. https://www.theguardian.com/books/2015/apr/25toni-morrison-books-interview-god-help-the-child.

Holt, Brianna. "What They Mean When They Say You're 'Not Social Enough' at Work." *Zora Medium*, January 28, 2021. https://zora.medium.com/black-women-dont-have-the-freedom-to-be-introverts-at-work-ed17fd795aee.

hooks, bell. *All About Love: New Visions*. New York: William Morrow and Company, 2021.

Hughes, Langston. "Salvation." *The Big Sea*. Farrar, Straus and Giroux, 1993.

Kincaid, Jamaica. *The Autobiography of My Mother*. New York: Plume, 1997.

Lee, Terrance. *Quiet Voice Fearless Leader: 10 Principles for Introverts to Awaken the Leader Inside*. Frenchtown Publishing, 2021.

McWatt, Tessa. *Shame on Me: An Anatomy of Race and Belonging*. Penguin Random House Canada, 2020.

Montañez, Rachel. "Here's How to Actually Help Women of Color With Burnout." *Forbes*, February 21, 2021. https://www.forbes.com/sites/rachelmontanez/2021/02/21/heres-how-to-actually-help-women-of-color-with-burn-out/?sh=59ae0eb51167.

Muccino, Gabriele, dir. *Pursuit of Happyness*. Sony Picture Releasing, 2006.

Perry, Andre M. "Black Men Have a Masculinity Problem and It's Hurting Their Kids' Sexual health." *The Washington Post*, October 8, 2014. https://www.washingtonpost.com /posteverything/wp/2014/10/08/how-dads-are-ruining -black-teens-sexual-health.

Pointer, Ashley. "Trap Music: Where It Came from and Where It's Going." Take Note: Inspiration for Music Makers. https://online.berklee.edu/takenote/trap-music-where -it-came-from-and-where-its-going.

Roderique, Hadiya. "Black on Bay Street: Hadiya Roderique Had It All. But Still Could Not Fit In." *The Globe and Mail*, November 4, 2017, updated February 22, 2023. https:// www.theglobeandmail.com/news/toronto/hadiya -roderique-black-on-bay-street/article36823806.

Roderique, Hadiya. "The Case for Black Joy." *FASHION*, February 21, 2019. https://fashionmagazine.com/flare /the-case-for-black-joy.

Rodgers, Rachel. *We Should All Be Millionaires: A Woman's Guide to Earning More, Building Wealth and Gaining Economic Power*. New York: HarperCollins Leadership, 2021.

Shakur, Prince. "Frank Ocean, *Moonlight*, and the New Era of Queer Black Men in Pop Culture." *Teen Vogue*, March 26, 2019. https://www.teenvogue.com/story /new-era-queer-black-men-pop-culture.

Taylor, Sonya R. *The Body Is Not an Apology: The Power of Radical Self-love*. Oakland: Berrett-Koehler Publishers, 2018.

Tejada, Angelica. "Enough Is Enough, Give Black TikTok Creators the Recognition They Deserve." *The Ticker*, April 15, 2021. https://theticker.org/3577/opinions/enough-is -enough-give-black-tiktok-creators-the-recognition-they -deserve.

Thompson, Krissah. "We Asked Black Mothers How They Find Their Joy. This Is What They Said." *The Washington Post*, September 20, 2019. https://www.washingtonpost .com/lifestyle/2019/09/20/we-asked-black-mothers-how -they-find-their-joy-this-is-what-they-said.

Warland, Betsy. *Breathing the Page: Reading the Act of Writing*. Toronto: Cormorant Books, 2010.

Williams, Ian. *Disorientation: Being Black in the World*. Toronto: Random House Canada, 2021.